The Yoga Portal

Rosamund J. Webster

In the writing of this book, every effort has been made to obtain copyright permission for any quotations, excerpts or pictures.

Copyright © Rosamund Webster 2013
All rights reserved.

ISBN-13:978-1490383910
ISBN-10:1490383913

The Yogal Portal

For

Peter, Jay and Petya

"The best way to make your dreams come true is to wake up."

~ Paul Valery

Foreword

In her book, The Yoga Portal, Rosamund suggests that some students are drawn to learn yoga due to the philosophy and traditions underpinning this ancient practice. I am one of those students. However, I feel it takes a special kind of person to inspire a student to embrace the art, science and spiritual practice of yoga. I had tried several yoga teachers prior to meeting Rosamund purely by chance. Her gentle, spiritual yet grounded approach to her life and practice as a yoga teacher resonated with my personal philosophy and outlook.

I have been fortunate to learn meditation as well as yoga with Rosamund and these have been life-changing experiences. As an Emotional Therapeutic Counsellor, I needed a teacher with a balanced approach who could enable me to support myself while supporting others. Rosamund is gentle but firm, calm though motivated, kind yet strong. Energetically, I find a sense of balance difficult to achieve yet in Rosamund's deeply calming presence, I always find space within myself to reconnect.

Rosamund's book is truly a reflection of her beliefs and values. When reading it I can just hear her reassuring and encouraging tones. Her description of the underpinning concepts of yoga are interesting, non-pretentious and un-mysterious, making yoga an accessible and inspiring practice for all. I will be using this wonderful book to guide and inspire me on my yogic journey and would recommend it to anyone who is drawn to the transformational practice of yoga.

Kate Moriarty
BSc. Hons., MFETC
EMOTIONAL THERAPEUTIC COUNSELLOR

The Yogal Portal

Acknowledgements

Loving and grateful thanks to my editor, Anne Marks, for her scrupulous attention to detail and skilful support in helping me to give birth to this project.

Much gratitude and thanks to my husband Peter, who painstakingly created the pictures and listened to all my ponderings about every aspect of this book.

I received much needed encouragement from Jay, my son, who also listened, gave excellent feedback and added wind to my sails. I am so grateful for the support of Petya and Alex whose excellent interpretation of the postures add such grace and visual interest to the book.

To all my teachers, those that I've worked with, those who have prepared the ground before me and those whom I've met only through the medium of their books and whose written work continues to support and inspire me - I am truly grateful. Thanks in particular to Maura Sills of Karuna Institute and Phil Young and Morag Campbell of Masterworks.

Thanks to all my students from whom I've learned as much as I've taught. Their constancy and Tikki's questions have contributed to this book.

The Yogal Portal

Contents

	Page
My Story	xiii
Yoga and the Subtle Energy System	1
The Energy Fields of the Body	10
The Koshas	12
The Nadis	15
Granthis and Bhandas	17
Grantis	17
Bandhas	18
Maha Bandha	19
Throat Lock	20
Abdominal Lock	21
Root Lock	21
The Chakras	23
Diagram of the Chakras and Elements	30
The Five Elements	31
Earth Element	33
Water Element	38
Fire Element	42
Air Element	47
Ether Element	52
The Postures	57
Mountain Pose	58

Contents

	Page
The Postures (cont'd.)	
Dancer Pose	62
Triangle Pose	66
Warrior Pose	70
Tree Pose	74
Eagle Pose	78
Shiva's Dance Pose	82
Gate Pose	86
Downward Facing Dog Pose	90
Cobra Pose	94
Hero's Pose	100
Boat Pose	104
Twist of Sage Pose	107
Bridge Pose	111
Bow Pose	115
Meditation	120
Breathing	126
Breathing Techniques	128
You Can Never Speak Up Too Often	130

The Yogal Portal

Star Pose

"You are an aperture through which the universe
is looking at and exploring itself."
~ Alan Watts

The Dream of the Earth
by Thomas Berry
(An Excerpt)

"The story of the universe is the story of the emergence of a galactic system in which each new level of expression emerges through the urgency of self-transcendence. Hydrogen in the presence of some millions of degrees of heat emerges into helium. After the stars take shape as oceans of fire in the heavens, they go through a sequence of transformations. Some eventually explode into the stardust out of which the solar system and the earth take shape. Earth gives unique expression of itself in its rock and crystalline structure and in the variety and splendour of living forms, until humans appear as the moment in which the unfolding universe becomes conscious of itself.

"The human emerges not only as an earthling, but also as a worldling. We bear the universe in our beings as the universe bears us in its being. The two have a total presence to each other and to that deeper mystery out of which both the universe and ourselves have emerged."

My Story

*"Perhaps another way of looking at it is that instead of trying to force my surfboard in a certain direction,
I was learning to let the wave do the work for me."*

~ Kristen N. Fox

Like most of us, I encountered my share of bumps along the road of Life and about five years ago, one of these was a diagnosis of arthritis. Since then, I am often asked how it is that I can still teach yoga. This question is usually followed very quickly by a second query along the lines of:

> "If a health-conscious person like you can have arthritis then what hope is there for us ordinary folk?"

While this response is understandable, it is, nonetheless, an incomplete way of looking at ourselves. A diagnosis is not nearly as important as what we choose to do with it. It is a bump along Life's highway and the thing about bumps is that closer examination usually reveals important information about them. Illness in any part of our bodies indicates that homeostasis has been compromised. The arthritic "bump" in my case was my body's way of communicating to me that something was out of whack; it was not receiving everything it needed to maintain its equilibrium.

It is very easy, amid the stresses of modern life with its fondness for multitasking, to ignore subtle feedback from our bodies and to find ourselves ill and unable to cope as we did before. How we can best support ourselves through a period of change becomes a very important question during such times.

The way I chose to deal with it entailed a shift of focus away from the debilitating symptoms and towards what I have always held close. I had my first formal Hatha Yoga lesson three decades ago and fell in love with this system which addresses not only issues of the body but the mind and spirit as well. I am tremendously grateful to have been introduced to yoga and continue to reap its benefits. Over the years, whenever health challenges popped up, I have used it along with meditation as a rope ladder. I hold on and climb out of whatever pit seeks to limit me and my abilities.

This often means embracing change, making adjustments, using modifications and adaptations while working beneath my abilities until I regain my strength and am able to rebalance the disrupted elements.

Part of my self-imposed therapy over the years has been to make notes of whatever pearls of wisdom I'd gathered along with any discoveries I'd made in my journey through the yoga portal. I'm so happy that I did because now I can share my love for this discipline with you.

Come, the portal awaits.

The Yogal Portal

Yoga and the Subtle Energy System

It has been found in Sacred Geometry that certain shapes can reach deeply into our unconscious and bring about changes in our state of mind or being. You may have noticed this yourself as you practise yoga.

Putting our bodies into a variety of shapes has a corresponding effect on our psychology. Certain shapes correlate with our personal symbols whose psychological significance and meaning subsequently impacts our understanding of ourselves. Assuming The Mountain Pose, for example, is often enough to make us feel stronger both in body and mind.

The philosophers and scientists of ancient Greece and much of Europe, as early as c. 47 and continuing beyond the 17th century, have believed in the geometric underpinnings of the cosmos. They thought that certain numbers carried an intrinsic meaning, aside from their ordinary use for counting or calculating and that plane figures such as the polygons, triangles, squares, hexagons, and so forth, were related to the number three and the triangle, and that these shapes or figures carried even more emotional value than the numbers themselves, because they were visual.

Symbolically, squares and rectangles represent the earth, integrity, universal order and the material realm. They infer structure and even containment. In many eastern religions, The square is often paired with its opposite number, the circle, a geometric figure whose mystique has pervaded many disciplines outside of mathematics with its reference to the sun, moon and eternity.

In the religions of Hinduism and Buddhism, mandalas are often used as an aid to meditation and the concept known as *the squaring of the circle* (shown in the drawing below) is of a well-known mandala which seeks to convey the idea of reconciliation between heaven and earth and the integration of polar opposites.

A diagrammatic drawing of the mandala Sri Yantra, showing the outside square, with four T-shaped gates, and the central circle.

The Yogal Portal

Borobudur Temple Stupa Ruin in Yogyakarta Java, Indonesia.

Throughout Asia, stupas of different designs and decoration can be seen. They are fine examples of Buddhist artistic architecture and started off housing the relics of the dead devotees but then moved on to contain teachings, writings and mantras. Over time their shapes became more elaborate and changes in design occurred but the essential sacred significance has always been retained. It is thought that the different shapes of the stupas are meant to convey the five elements of earth, water, fire, air and ether.

The circle is a mathematical concept of enormous importance and serves also as a symbol for unity and infinity. In alchemy, the circle offers protective powers when one stands within it. When we assume the pose of tranquility in yoga, we place ourselves within a circle as we do when we are in wind-relieving posture or child pose. Throughout the ages architects, mathematicians and cultures the world over, have used symbolic language to enhance their communications. Its natural application in yoga lends new meaning to, and furthers our understanding of, the concept of body language.

In Star Pose, at the beginning of this book, the body is in the shape of a square or rectangle (if one draws an imaginary line from fingertips to toes) and stands poised within a subtle energetic circle similar to Leonardo da Vinci's Vitruvian Man which represents a perfectly balanced human.

In the Trikonasana/Triangle posture, there is a downward (masculine) and upward (feminine) triangle. When these two shapes are inverted upon each other to form a hexagram, it becomes representative of the union of opposites or a merging of spirit (air element) with the physical (earth element), aptly portraying the effect of the alchemical principle: "As above, so below" as an indication of how changes in one affects the other.

Positioning our bodies into these geometrical shapes whose symbolic meanings have permeated the collective unconscious since time immemorial, has a corresponding effect on our psychology at a deep level. Certain shapes have the power to evoke emotional responses in us and can become our personal archetypes carrying the weight of their psychological significance and meaning; imparting their own story.

The words "Hatha Yoga" themselves carry a powerful message. *Ha* translates to Sun, *tha* to Moon and *Yoga* to join or unity. Literally, the unity of Sun (masculine principle) and Moon (feminine principle). In Jungian psychology, these are referred to as the anima and animus. The anima is the feminine aspect of the male psyche and the animus the masculine aspect of the female psyche). Both sexes share these aspects. As we practise yoga, over time we are led towards the kundalini experience which brings these male and female energies into balance, harmony and blissful unity.

The subtle energy system, which is part of yogic philosophy, offers a holistic paradigm for understanding ourselves and the world around us which consists of:

- Nadis
- Chakras
- The Five Elements
- The Granthis, and
- The Koshas

The five elements of earth, water, fire, air and ether which are present in the outer world are also represented in our mind/body phenomena and as we grow in our understanding of this system, we begin to see how the strengths and weaknesses of our personalities and health are influenced when the chakras and elements become imbalanced, depleted or excessive due to lifestyle choices, bad habits, erroneous attitude, accidents, ill health, poor dietary choices and environmental factors. To create a free flow of energy throughout this subtle energy system, the Hatha Yoga model proposes a regime of:

- posture practice (asanas)
- breathing techniques and practices (pranayama)
- positioning of the hands and the body in order to establish powerful and special energy patterns similar to electrical circuits (mudras)
- the use of locks to direct energy (bandhas)
- appropriate diet

Students come to Yoga for a variety of reasons. Some seek it out due to health problems or as a result of a decision to embrace a new lifestyle choice. Others are sent by their doctors or health care practitioners.

Then there are those who come because they are attracted to the physical aspects of the posture work or are drawn to the tradition and the philosophy behind it.

To think of yoga simply as an alternative exercise routine is to diminish all that this discipline has to offer. It is so much more than merely practising physical postures. It also opens up mental pathways whose benefits reach far beyond the mat. In the pursuit of these pathways, I have found that the most important tools are:

- **Intention**
  Establishes purpose and adds meaning to our activity.

- **Attention**
  Adds focus and concentration as we use our minds like an aperture that we narrow at will to encompass only what it is we want to look at in the moment.

- **Awareness**
  Expands our minds and heightens our senses allowing us to make the connection between our inflexible attitudes and our unyielding joints.

We live in a world constantly bombarded with information and misinformation. As well, we are flooded with colossal amounts of advertising and merchandising in increasingly consumer-driven and materially-obsessed societies. In the midst of this turmoil, yoga, if practiced skillfully, can provide an experience of peace and a path for transformation.

As the Upanishad says:

> Lead Us From the Unreal To the Real,
> Lead Us From Darkness To Light,
> Lead Us From Death To Immortality,
> Let There Be Peace Peace Peace.
>
> – Brihadaranyaka Upanishad 1.3.28

The philosophies of Buddhism, Taoism and Yoga all encourage us to be attentive in the present moment. The practice of yoga, a highly self-reflective process, wakes us up and jolts us out of our habitual patterns of cravings, aversions, addictions and greed, allowing us to let go of old modes of thinking and ways of being.

When we are successful in raising the level of our awareness it becomes a portal to another way of being; another way of seeing ourselves and the world.

The Warrior postures, for example, are instrumental in helping us to face our demons in their various forms of expression as anger, envy or obsessiveness. Yoga offers us an opportunity to create, by our own efforts, a life for ourselves that is healthy, joyful and full of vitality. It is a means by which we can approach the Self at our own pace and learn about ourselves through our own personal symbols and metaphors which inevitably rise to consciousness as we move through the postures.

Many students, as well as teachers, come to yoga with ailments, choosing to work through their bouts of ill health with the understanding that health is a dynamic process and not merely the absence of illness. More often than not, they discover that it is possible for joy to be found and experienced in the midst of difficulties and hardship.

Knowing that we can openly engage with whatever maladies we may encounter as part of our earthly journey; find relief and a space to hold it all; the pain *and* the pleasure, without pushing away from the direct experience of it, lends vitality and a sense of balance to our existence.

The Energy Fields of the Body

As a teacher of Hatha Yoga, my approach to the body encompasses a wider perspective.

Our bodies are a complex of atoms and sub-atomic energy fields in a process of flux. Our organs vibrate at different frequencies and our bodies have many pulses. In Ayurvedic and Vibrational Medicine, the practitioners are trained to diagnose an illness based on the differing pulses or frequencies of energy coming from the human body. Doctors are trained to read ECG feedback to interpret the electrical impulses of our hearts. If we are ready to assume the responsibility of healing ourselves, then understanding who or what it is that we are attempting to restore can only be beneficial.

The body is not merely that which we can see. It also includes the subtle body and all its energy fields, some of which are: The koshas or sheaths, the chakras and nadis, the meridians or long line currents and the upward/downward facing triangles.

If we are mindful in our asana practice and bring the key tools of intention and awareness to the work, we can bear witness to the changes taking place through our bodies and into these energy fields. We can observe how the interplay influences our consciousness and come to appreciate how our yoga mat can become a place of awakening and transformation.

Let us take a closer look at some of these energy fields as they are defined in the yoga paradigm.

THE KOSHAS

The Sanskrit word kosha means sheath. In Vedantic philosophy, a kosha is one of five layers of humanity, the nature of which encompasses physical as well as psychological aspects that function as one holistic system.

The Kosha system refers to these different aspects as layers of subjective experience ranging from the dense physical body to the more subtle (psychological) levels of emotions, mind and spirit. Together, all aspects make up our subjective experience of being alive.

The five layers of the koshas are:

- ❖ **Annamaya Kosha**
  The sheath of the physical body, nourished by food.

- ❖ **Pranamaya Kosha**
  The sheath of prana or vital principle. This is the force that brings life into the body and mind.

- ❖ **Manomaya Kosha**
  The sheath of the mind.

- ❖ **Vijnanamaya Kosha**
  The sheath of wisdom.

- ❖ **Anandamaya Kosha**

    The sheath of bliss. This sheath surrounds the Self which is joy, rapture, bliss.

These koshas can be experienced through meditation or yogic practices.

The Yogal Portal

DIAGRAM OF THE KOSHAS

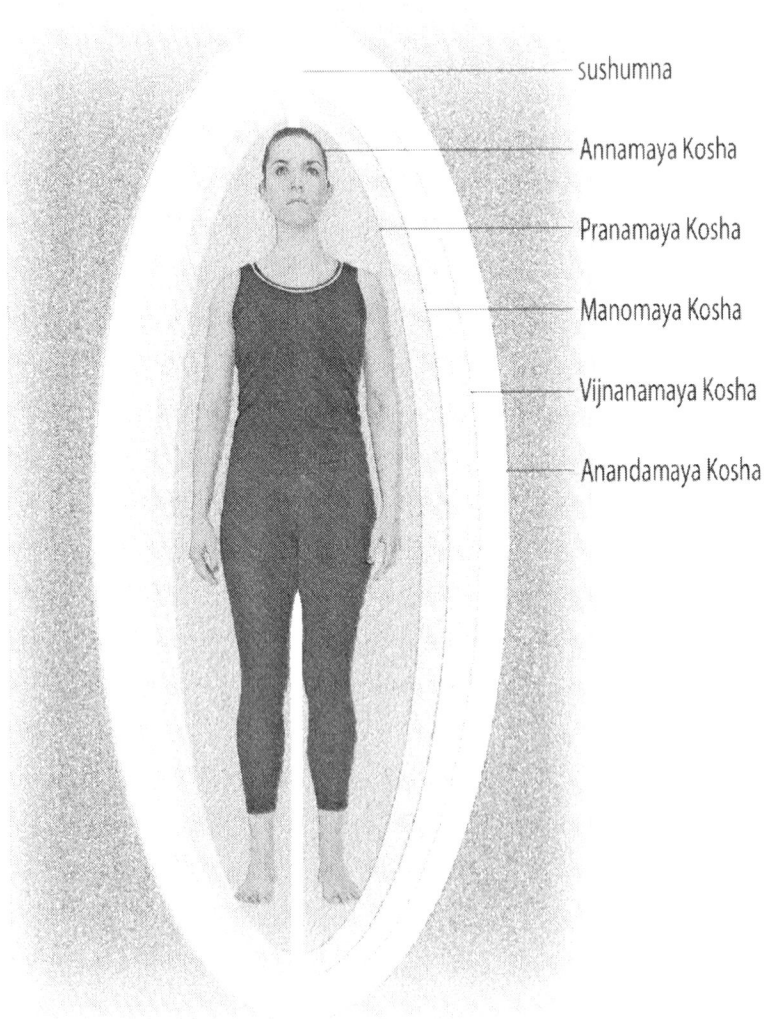

THE NADIS

A nadi is a stream or a channel of consciousness of which there are many. These conduct the movement of prana, chi, life force or energy through the body and connect at special points of intensity called the chakras.

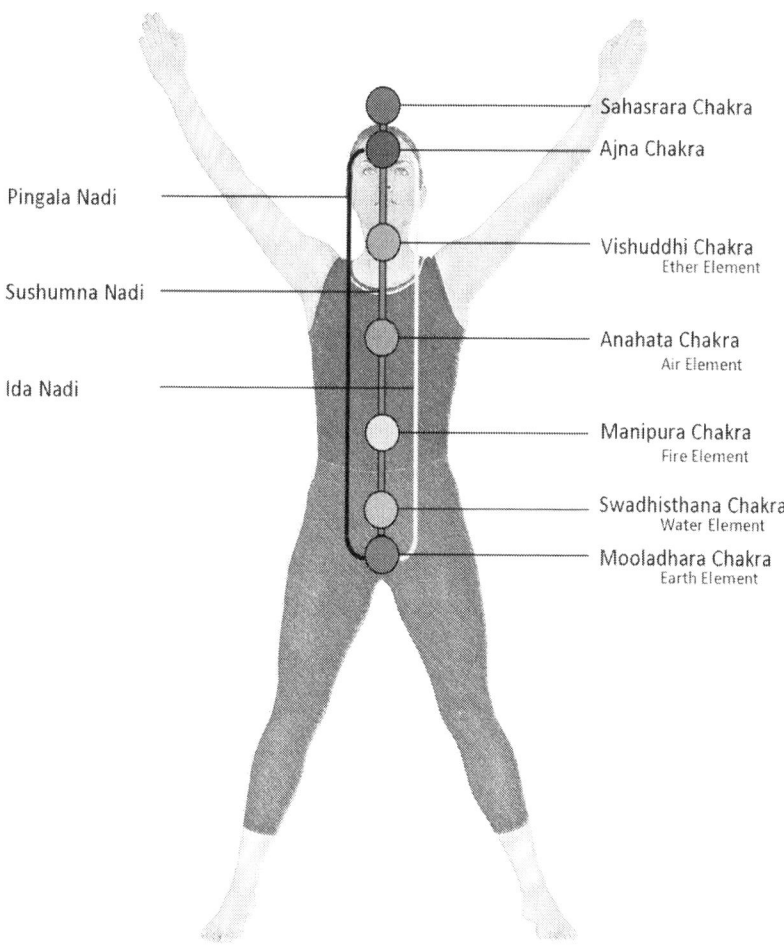

The three main nadis are Sushumna, Ida and Pingala. These nadis also embrace the meridians in acupuncture and the long line currents in polarity therapy.

Sushumna lies within the spinal column and is neutral. It is said to run from the base of the spine to the base of skull, joining the crown chakra.

Ida and Pingala alternate along the spinal column where they form chakras until they reach the Ajna chakra at the brow centre ending in the right and left nostrils. Ida is a feminine current of energy or channel of consciousness closely associated with life-giving and creative principles. This feminine principle originates on the left side of the body and is often referred to as the Lunar energy.

Pingala is the masculine principle which originates on the right hand side of the body and is referred to as the solar energy. The masculine principle is vital, outgoing, purifying and creative. When we practise Alternate Nostril Breathing we are balancing the Ida and Pingala nadis, bringing the mind and body into a state of equilibrium.

GRANTHIS AND BHANDAS

Granthis

A granthi is a psychic or energetic knot of which there are three:

- ❖ Brahma granthi
- ❖ Vishnu granthi
- ❖ Rudra granthi

These knots impede or slow down the free movement of prana being transmuted along the Sushumna nadi or channel. The granthi's role is one of imparting prudence and a form of restraint, allowing the chakras to become established in the new frequency of energy flowing through it.

The Brahma granthi (knot) lies in between the Mooladahara and Swadhisthana Chakras. These granthis inhibit the rise of kundalini until the knot is released. Prior to its release, the restricted energy can manifest as restlessness and agitation which can prevent progress as we venture into deeper practices of yoga.

Before the Vishnu granthi knot, located between Manipura and Anahata Chakras, is released, we are caught up with self-identity and less inclined to be compassionate.

The Rudra Granthi knot lies between the Vishuddhi and Ajna Chakras and when it has been untied the old ego standpoints no longer hold sway. Kundalini is free to rise bringing us the gifts of joy, loving-kindness and grace.

Bandhas

A bandha is a lock you apply in yoga practice to engage and stimulate the subtle energies to move from the lower to the higher chakras where they can then be transmuted.

There are four bandhas:

- ❖ mula bandha

- ❖ uddiyana bandha

- ❖ jalandhara bandha

- ❖ maha bandha

The application of a bandha is practised if one is seeking to obtain spiritual insight, transcendence or liberation. In yoga, a bandha would be used to stimulate energy in areas of the granthi in order to encourage the movement of kundalini along the Sushumna nadi. The granthis cannot be coerced into opening; the necessary psychological preparedness has to be done before a shift in consciousness takes place.

For example, when you apply mula bandha you are connected to the Brahma granthi. In applying Uddiyana bandha you are connected to Vishnu granti and the application of Jalandhara bandha connects you to the Rudra granthi.

In Maha Bandha, the three locks:

- ❖ Jalandhara Bandha – throat lock
- ❖ Uddiyana Bandha – abdominal lock
- ❖ Mula Bandha – root lock

are applied during an external retention of the breath.

Maha Bandha

Jalandhara Bandha

Uddiyana Bandha

Mula Bandha

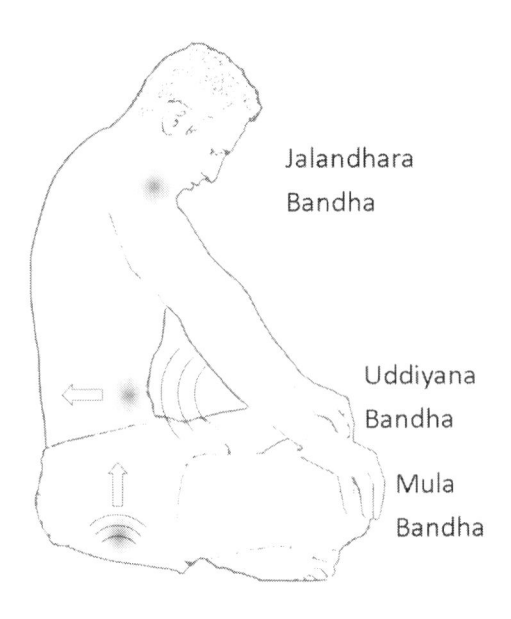

If you feel ready to try these locks, here are the steps that need to be followed:

Throat Lock
(Jalandhara Bandha)

1. Sit in a comfortable cross legged position. If you need to lift your hips to be more comfortable, use a yoga block.

2. Placing hands on knees, close the eyes, lengthen through the back, head in line with the spine.

3. Breathe in deeply and breathe out deeply retaining the breath externally.

4. Apply Jalandhara Bandha (Throat Lock) by dropping the chin into the top of the chest.

Abdominal Lock
(Uddiyana Bandha)

5. Bend the head forward bringing the chin to the chest.

6. Press down on the knees, straightening the arms while lifting the shoulders upwards.

7. Apply Uddiyana Bandha - (Abdominal Lock) by contracting the abdominal muscles inwards and upwards.

Root Lock
(Mula Bandha)

8. Take your attention to the perineal floor, contract the muscles and draw this area up.

9. Apply Mula Bandha (Root Lock).

10. Hold these three bandhas without straining for as long as you are comfortable.

11. Release in reverse order: root lock, abdominal lock and then chin lock.

12. Inhale slowly and deeply.

Maha bandha can be practised in reverse order by applying the followings:

    Mula

    Uddiyana

    Jalandhara bandhas

In the release stage, first release:

    Jalandhara

    Uddiyana

    Mula bandha

These locks can also be practised individually.

The Chakras

*"When we get to the level of atoms,
the landscape is not one of solid objects moving around
each other like partners in a dance, following predictable steps.
Subatomic particles are separated by huge gaps, making every atom more
than 99.99 percent empty space."*

~ Deepak Chopra

Chakras are part of the subtle energy system, although unseen, they are just as important as the seen systems in the body and the world around us. A modern teacher, Tenzin Wangyal Rinpoche, uses a computer analogy to help us understand the role that chakras play, he explains that the main chakras are like hard drives. Each hard drive has many files and one of the files is always open in each of the chakras, no matter how "closed" that particular chakra may be. What is displayed by the file, shapes our experience.

A chakra is a spinning circle of subtle energy which lies along the spinal column forming a pathway through which we can increase our level of awareness and come to a better understanding of our personal psychology.

Of the seven main chakras, five have elements. These are all linked to various nerve networks and interwoven structures, the nervous system and the gross body. This vortex of energy is always there but because our attention is often located elsewhere, we often remain unaware of it. Also, at that level, it is not always possible to process all of the information at the speed at which it occurs.

Each chakra houses an element which can be seen as a stage in life that we all go through. We express our personality, health, strengths and weaknesses via this energy pathway. It can also be seen as a map of how we move through the day, the month or the year. We may have one or two chakras in which we feel most competent and comfortable and this becomes our way of interacting with the world. Balancing these elements is an approach towards becoming more fully acquainted with our humanity.

In the Jungian system of psychology, the theory of Psychological Type proposes the existence of two dichotomous pairs of cognitive functions:

- ❖ the "rational" (judging) functions: *thinking* and *feeling, and*

- ❖ the "irrational" (perceiving) functions: *sensing* and *intuition*

This model states that for every person each of the

functions is expressed primarily in either an introverted or extraverted form. However, it is not my purpose to detail this system but merely to show that these constructs for understanding ourselves in the world are employed elsewhere and that the yogic system reflects one such overlap.

The Jungian model illustrates that the *Sensation* type processes experience through the physical senses; through what can be touched and seen; things that are concrete. An *Intuitive* type comprehends experience through that which is unseen or abstract and is more likely to follow hunches. The *Thinking* type views experience through a logical, measured and reasonable style while the *Feeling* type interprets experience via a process of empathy and consideration for all parties before making decisions.

In the Yoga paradigm we have the five elements of earth, water, fire, air and ether which make up the universe of which we are a part. In this system, each element influences our typology.

Through the use of symbols and a comparison between the yoga paradigm and the Jungian model of typology, one can easily see how the Earth element could be linked to *Sensation*, Water to *Feeling*, Fire to *Intuitive* and Air to *Thinking*, thereby creating a synthesis between the model of the west and ancient, eastern yogic principles.

The ether, while an element in its own right, may be construed as the space within which all the other elements rest and have their existence. It is a place of spaciousness and integration.

These elements then express and manifest themselves through a Balanced or Imbalanced mode. No one is a pure type. A person may clearly demonstrate competence in two or three elements and then experience difficulties in one or two. It is also possible for one of the elements to be completely on the blind side.

None of these elements or types is better in quality than any other. The model is a tool that serves to help us recognize how we function within the space-time continuum. It is another step in the journey towards understanding the functions of our personality and ultimately transports us to an expanded level of awareness. From this new vantage point, we may realize that there are more choices available to us about how we could be.

If, in the course of practising yoga at this level, we find that there are two elements we are competent in using and one that trips us up, then our task becomes the harmonious integration of the elements, along with their lessons, within our personalities; all the while dancing skillfully with the energies present at that moment. Through our practice, these shortcomings or neuroses are engaged and transformed into growth and maturity.

Given that we are spacious creatures why is it that we hold ourselves so tightly? When we are in love we meet the world in quite an expanded state. Yet, maintaining the initial euphoria and expansion does not come naturally to us and we are unable to hold on to it as we pursue our daily activities.

Living in a world of opposites, we can understand the concept of liberation because we know the meaning of bondage; and joy because we know sadness. We move from expansion to contraction and vice versa in a natural cycle. We often get caught up in the illusion that we are our beliefs, thoughts, opinions, likes and dislikes. With more awareness of our moment to moment process we may notice that one of the most important things we can do for ourselves is to create a space between our shapes and our Self.

If we compare the yogic paradigm by overlaying it onto another well-known western theoretical diagram, i.e., Maslow's Hierarchy of Needs, a picture emerges of the different stages that occur as we move through our lives over any given period of time.

Looking at this triangle, starting at the bottom and working our way upwards, we can see that when we are babies and young children we predominantly experience some aspects of earth and water. As we approach and grow into the teen years, we experience more of air and water. It is important to note, however, that as we move through the various phases, incidents that occur in the ether level will undoubtedly colour our psycho/spiritual experiences.

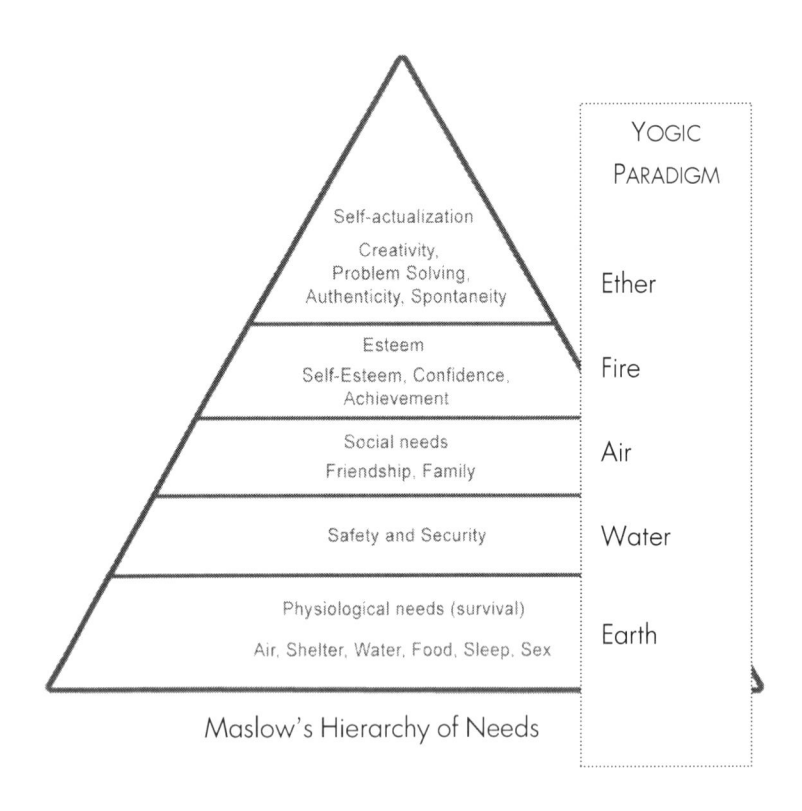

```
                    YOGIC
                  PARADIGM

   Self-actualization
      Creativity,
   Problem Solving,              Ether
 Authenticity, Spontaneity

      Esteem
 Self-Esteem, Confidence,        Fire
     Achievement

    Social needs
  Friendship, Family             Air

  Safety and Security            Water

 Physiological needs (survival)
Air, Shelter, Water, Food, Sleep, Sex   Earth
```

Maslow's Hierarchy of Needs

As young adults we come around again to earth and water experiences, maturing as we move through fire and air once more, developing our capacity for ether experiences.

This triangle does not hold only an upward trajectory. It is a continuum in and through which we move during the different stages of life. However, it is clear that if the base is not solid then the movement upwards becomes shaky. There are many stops and starts along the way depending on our circumstances. If, perchance, we encounter unemployment, loss of home or family, very little energy is left for the pursuit of personal liberation.

THE CHAKRAS
AND
ELEMENTS

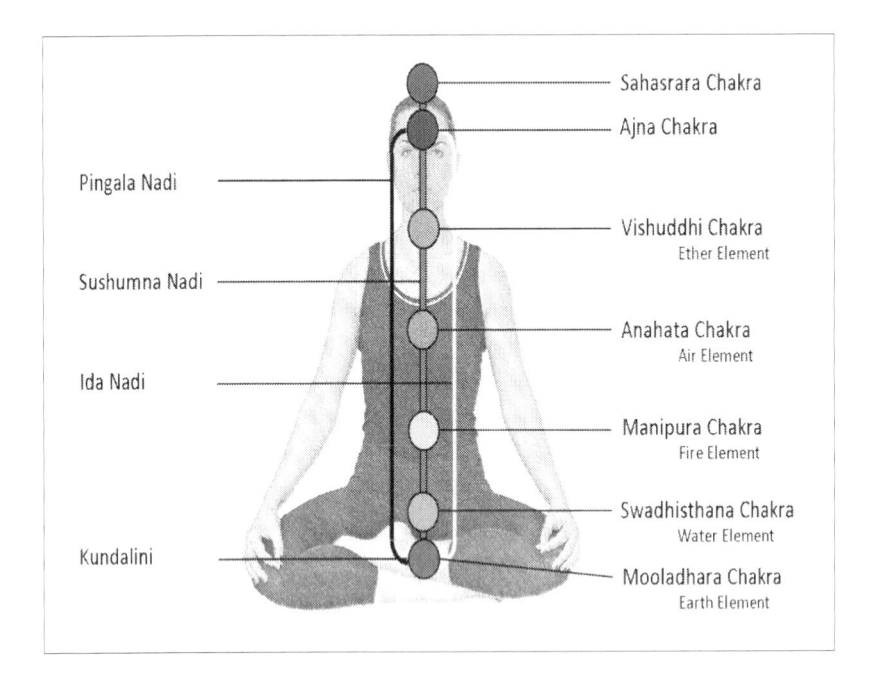

- Sahasrara Chakra
- Ajna Chakra
- Pingala Nadi
- Vishuddhi Chakra
  Ether Element
- Sushumna Nadi
- Anahata Chakra
  Air Element
- Ida Nadi
- Manipura Chakra
  Fire Element
- Swadhisthana Chakra
  Water Element
- Kundalini
- Mooladhara Chakra
  Earth Element

The Five Elements

"Be at least as interested in what goes on inside you as what happens outside. If you get the inside right, the outside will fall into place."

~ Eckhart Tolle

Different cultures have developed different ways of classifying the elements. In addition to the classical four of earth, water, fire and air identified by the ancient Greeks, the Hindu and Yogic system added ether. To all of these, the Chinese added wood and metal.

The better we understand these elements and their relationship to the chakras, the better we will be able to use our yoga postures to help us attain optimal health in body, mind and spirit.

All five elements exist in all five chakras. What this means is that within each chakra there is to be found a component of each of the five elemental levels of energy and each element corresponds to a different structure in the body, for example, the earth element corresponds to solid structures, such as bones, flesh, skin, tissues, and hair, and the water element to saliva, urine and all the other liquid aspects of the physical body[1]. When the elements are out of balance with one another, disease and suffering may occur.

If we look at the following descriptions and qualities of the various elements we will see just how closely intertwined they are with the chakras and how the manifestation of our humanity is affected in both our inner and outer worlds when these are balanced or imbalanced.

---

[1] Maggie Begley, www.fundamentalfield.com

The Earth Element Housed in the Mooladahara (Root) Chakra

"All that we are is the result of what we have thought. The mind is everything. What we think we become."

~ Gautama Buddha

Location: Perineum/Coccyx, perineal floor, Coccygeal plexus

Function: Survival, self-preservation, life-force, foundation, creativity.

Sense: Smell

Body and Astrological Relationships:

    Musculoskeletal system
    Neck (Taurus)
    Bowels/Large intestines (Virgo)
    Knee (Capricorn)

Body Type: Block-like, stout, sturdy, thick neck, robust health.

Qualities:

> Matters relating to finance, the world, law, security, practicality, support, patience, groundedness, survival, robust health, self-preservation, creating and imparting bounty.

Energetic Imbalances:

> Overly reliant on structure and routine, narrowness of vision, limitations, bounded, selfish, sluggishness, inertia, lack of groundedness, fear, laziness, tension in spine, constipation, haemorrhoids, sciatica, skeletal problems.

The Earth-dominated personality meets the world concerned with establishing solid foundations and possessions. They are very supportive and good at establishing structure where it is needed. They work diligently to achieve satisfaction with their attendant financial rewards and bring structure and attention to detail in their undertakings. A negative manifestation can result in miserly, scrooge-like behaviour when it swings into an addiction towards the acquisition of wealth at the expense of others. In the Mooladahara Chakra lies kundalini which, when activated, can move up through the chakras bringing integration and unity.

In the pursuit of earning a wage and creating a bank account wealth may be confused with having money. Their strength lies in their ability for consistency, stability and substance. They make good teachers, lawyers, financiers and police officers.

When this element is allowed to reach extreme imbalance sociopathic behaviour is likely to manifest. We can see an example of this on the current world stage with the collapse of some large financial houses and the sense of entitlement of their executives to huge, unjustifiable sums of money.

The established infrastructures of society: government, the legal system, banking, law and order, all reflect the earth element and presently, we are in a position to observe many of these institutions experience extreme turbulence while the earth element goes through a period of dissolution in order to re-establish a new framework.

Chakras and the elements influence our health, life issues, behaviour and attitudes and manifest themselves in that space where we meet the world. A fire type personality can manifest miserly, penny-pinching behaviour if they are experiencing an earth element imbalance. Fear and insecurity are the main issues this type would have to work with and depending on the individual; the issues could range from obsessions to mild feelings of fear and anxiety.

An excess of negative earth element could manifest in a restricted imagination, a narrow-minded and limited outlook on life. Taking a heavy-handed approach with and a lack of sensitivity for the emotions of others would be something to guard against. These attitudes create an imbalance in the earth element. To restore balance, it might be wise to seek comfort in the knowledge that we are all in a process of change and nothing lasts forever.

Many people deny or negate the importance of the base chakra and all the earth element has to offer but a simple adjustment in our attitude and the application of a little effort could help us strike a happy balance, neither neglecting nor obsessing about the issues.

When we pursue the upper chakras and dedicate most of our efforts towards spiritual and intellectual interests, choosing in the process, to treat the concept of capitalism with disdain, we fail to see that our creative abilities are severely hampered when we are unable to support ourselves or help anyone else. Consequently, the upper chakras become overblown while the lower chakras and elements remain unassimilated resulting in a lack of support or structure to continue the onward journey. Whatever we deny will eventually trip us up. In our quest for wholeness and balance, we need to understand that all the elements are equally important and contain within themselves their own creative energies, all of which have many gifts to offer.

Earth and water types are very closely related and can be prone to being overweight. In an effort to prevent their energies from becoming sluggish, two different types of exercise programmes, a high-energy routine such as zumba or net ball paired with a less intense discipline such as hatha yoga, tai-chi or power walking could be beneficial.

The Water Element
Housed in the Swadhisthana Chakra

*"Nothing is softer than water,
yet nothing can resist it."
~ Lao Tzu*

Location: Sacrum, lower abdomen, lumbosacral Plexus.

Function: Procreation, Sensuality, Sexuality, Pleasure, Creativity.

Sense: Taste

Body and Astrological relationships:

> Circulatory and Lymphatic system
> Breasts (Cancer)
> Reproductive organs (Scorpio)
> Feet (Pisces)

Body Type:

> Well developed body, soft fleshy padded body, padded pelvis, rounded.

Qualities: Sensitivity, Emotions, Procreation, Sexuality, Sensuality, Receiving, Giving, Caring, Patience, Support, Tolerance, Collaborative skills.

Energetic Imbalances:

>Attachments, holding on, inability to let go, overindulgence in food, sex, sexual problems, bladder problems, unruly emotions, jealousy, over-sensitivity, musculoskeletal problems.

A person who is Water-dominant will see the world as housing a plethora of pleasures. When this element is balanced the individual is usually happy, considerate and tolerant of others emotionally and sexually. They are fun-loving and can be the life and soul of the party, enjoying the company of others and are easy to be around. This type will be a good friend. Positive water has many gifts and like Aphrodite, we may discover through this element that sex can also be experienced as holy communion; a blessed sacrament.

When this element is out of balance, battles will generally ensue with issues of addiction, as susceptibility to drugs, sex, alcohol and gambling increase. Drugs have a variety of elemental qualities, some can make you sleepy, speedy, hallucinate or intense. A fire type may use a tranquilizing drug in order to 'come down.' An airy type may experiment with a hallucinogenic. Underlying all of this is a water element imbalance. The danger lies in seeing the pleasures as located *'out there'* without realizing that the capacity for pleasure resides within us.

The water element is equivalent to the realm of the unconscious, the part of the mind where psychic activity of which we are unaware takes place. It is where our repressions, trigger-points, unacknowledged feelings, etc., are housed - all of which prevent the individual from functioning efficiently or clearly as these forces exert their inner pressure. Many of us are reluctant to explore this area for various reasons the least not being that it is much easier to skim along on the surface rather than go looking for 'trouble'. Yet, if we look at the Water Element as a cycle in life we can see it for the growth stage that it is and are better able to understand how the development of positive water attributes is essential to the enjoyment of good relationships.

Yoga and Buddhism declare that we all have the capacity for lust, anger, jealousy, joy, kindness and serenity. In each moment we make a choice as to what we wish to cultivate. The more we cultivate the positive qualities the more they will arise which reinforces the importance of staying in the present moment and being aware of what is taking place in the here and now.

The water imbalance that we see portrayed in society as homelessness has more to do with our culture and our evolution as a society than with economic deficit. It is a reflection of our lack of connectedness to each other, to family and the community. A positive water element enhances our emotional intelligence and gives us a deep sense of unity with our families, community and ourselves. Relatedness brings heart into the centre of our thinking.

The Fire Element
Housed in the Manipura[2] Chakra

> "It is interesting to notice how some minds seem almost to create themselves, springing up under every disadvantage and working their solitary but irresistible way through a thousand obstacles."
>
> ~ Washington Irving

Location: At the Solar Plexus, behind the navel.

Function: Vitalizes sympathetic nervous system, digestive processes, metabolism, emotions, will power, empowerment, creativity.

Body and Astrological relationship:

> Digestive System
> Head/Eyes (Aries)
> Solar Plexus (Leo)
> Thighs (Sagittarius)

---

[2] Sanskrit word meaning city of jewels or jewelled lotus.

Body Type: Muscular, well-developed body. Athletic, sporty type (without exercise).

Sense: Sight

Qualities: Intense emotion, Laughter, Joy, Warmth, Passion, Radiance, Vitality, Directness, Intelligence, Insight, Self-discipline, Power, Authority, Intuition.

Energetic Imbalances:

Digestive problems, Eating disorders, Ulcers, Fatigue, Diabetes, Anger, Rage, and Impatience.

This chakra is the sacred pathway through which this element is activated, giving us insight into *the hidden city of jewels*. In other words, the activation of this element brings the light of awareness to our unconscious process.

The Fire-dominant person can be charismatic and dynamic, radiating warmth to their circle of friends and family. One of the life tasks for the Fire individual is the true development of power and will. This Fire type is concerned with developing their own authentic voice and empowering themselves and others. Imbued with good leadership skills they make good managers and directors.

The challenge for this type is to work with their anger creatively and to learn to have fun. When this element is out of balance, it can do untold damage. If self-discipline has not been developed their anger can move into rage and in extreme cases can be homicidal. They can present with a sense of aggrandizement.

Much carnage is committed daily through violence in our words and actions both in our personal lives and globally. Until we each realize the importance of bringing this energy into balance we will continue to inflict pain on ourselves and others.

The Fire types are often full of vitality and will work for a chosen cause without reward. When this element is balanced, this is the path of selfless service and karma yoga. However, because society rewards this behaviour, this type can easily become workaholic and it may be difficult to detect the addiction.

Fire is outward bound, warm and intense but it needs to learn about fun or risk burn out. This type greatly benefits from developing a practise of yoga, meditation, Tai Chi or Kum Nye to help them relax and rebalance their minds and bodies.

When we practise Right-Nostril Breathing (Sun breath or Surya Bheda pranayama), which stimulates the Pingala Nadi, we increase our vitality and sense of empowerment.

Skull shining or Kapalabhati Pranayama[3] is a breathing practice as well as a *shat kriya* - one of the six cleansing actions of hatha yoga. The defining characteristic of kapalabhati is a sharp, forceful exhalation from the abdomen, followed immediately by a passive, relaxed inhalation.

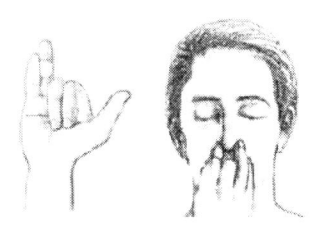

Surya Bedha Pranayama

With its emphasis on the exhalation, kapalabhati enhances elimination of volatile metabolic wastes and dispels sluggishness and congestion while engaging the seat of apana (downward moving energy) in the lower belly. This is an excellent morning practice that stimulates and balances the fire element.

In the Taoist, Japanese and Buddhist traditions this centre, called the Hara or Dan T'ien meaning 'the sea of energy' is considered a place of power. In martial arts and Tai Chi this is an important energy centre and there are similar breath practises to build chi in this area.

---

[3] YogaInternational.com © 2013

There is a link between this element and the development of athletics and sports and it is very likely that Muhammad Ali, the world famous boxer, and Bruce Lee, actor and renowned master of martial arts, would both have had a strong, well-developed Fire element in order to achieve what they did.

If we love what we do, work can be like music to the spirit. It can arouse our creativity, set us on fire, and bring us fulfilment. The more skilled we are at it the more we can rely on it to nurture and sustain us. Through work, it is possible to heal ourselves. At this level, when our work with the elements brings Ether into combination with Fire, work becomes a spiritual practice; a sacred ritual regardless of the nature of the particular job.

"When you work you are a flute through whose heart the whispering of the hours turns to music."

~ Khalil Gibran

Air Element
Housed in the Anahata[4] Chakra
(At the Anahata chakra the Air Element arises)

"Imagination is more important than knowledge."
~ Albert Einstein

Location: The heart centre. Situated around 4-5 thoracic vertebrae between the shoulder blades, Brachial plexus.

Function: Movement, motion, energizes the blood and body with life force energy/prana, blood circulation.

Body and Astrological relationships:

> Respiratory System
> Shoulders (Gemini)
> Kidneys (Libra)
> Ankles (Aquarius)

---

[4] Anahata, a Sanskrit word meaning 'unstuck', refers to the cosmic sounds heard everywhere but created by no-one, otherwise known as cosmic 'white' noise.

Body type: Tall, Thin, Long Limbs

Sense: Touch

Qualities: Compassion, understanding, balance, group consciousness, a sense of oneness with life, love, acceptance, movement.

Energetic Imbalances:

Asthma, heart diseases, blood-pressure problems, lung diseases, stuck in outmoded ideas and attitudes, sometimes disconnected from feelings, greed, acquisitive, nervous, anxious and agitated, cold in mind and body.

The Air Element-dominant person has a real gift for the imaginative and is usually helpful and open-hearted. They excel in the field of technology enjoying the world of the computers, internet and television. This element is capable of bringing us balance and integration, working with the elements below and above to transmute them into an expanded awareness of empathy and kindness. When combined with the Ether Element, the Air Element gathers momentum and reaches the crown chakra which leads to compassion and loving kindness.

The Air type has broad brush strokes, its beauty and creativity lies in its breadth and height, its lofty thinking and high ideals. However, this type is prone to nervous anxiety and there is often something sensitive or fragile about their structure or constitution. They can be tall, very slim and bordering on bony.

When the element is imbalanced the Air type can be nervy and anxious and become more caught up in thinking; disconnected from feeling. They can become ungrounded and evasive; their imagination can spiral downwards, and they may lose the ability to take responsibility for their lives. Without help and in extreme cases they can become apathetic and reclusive, slipping into schizoid-type problems.

One of our tasks as we evolve, is to shift our focus from the personal bond of love, understanding it as part of the journey which prepares us to experience *being* love.

> "Your task is not to seek for love,
> but merely to seek and find all the barriers
> within yourself that you have built against it."
>
> ~ Rumi

Huge expectations are created around our romantic idea of love as reflected in popular love songs and movies whose main themes revolve around the sentiment of 'I love you, do you love me?' as opposed to the expanded notion of 'How can I be love?' This is the element that will enable us to move from the personal to the transpersonal; to expand and experience the bigger picture. The work we can undertake with this element is to see it as an important part of our journey to the deeper experience of being more fully human.

A relationship is a vehicle through which we may experience many insights into heart and mind as we strive to become more conscious. Many of us think that the Air Element is about unconditional love but that is the work of the Crown Chakra. The process begins here and with the help of other elements, the Air Element is transmuted and prepared for its onward journey. When we are in love and experience the world from this expanded place, the journey which includes the breaking of the shell and the expansion of our awareness beyond our own parameters, has begun.

If this element is not balanced, individuals are overly concerned with me and mine. Acquisitions and greed are standard practice; shopping and other compulsions develop. This can often be remedied by creating a space through our yoga practice and meditation through which we can look beyond our stories to that place within each of us that is untouched by the trauma and suffering which we may experience in our daily lives.

We have seen from modern research and biofeedback

techniques that our thoughts influence our stress levels and our bodies in turn produce reactions that influence our thoughts. Going even beyond this notion of mind-body interaction, is the current thinking in the field of quantum mechanics that everything in the universe is connected and consequently, our worlds, both micro and macro become that much more complicated. It then becomes apparent that the clearer we can become in our thought processes, the more awareness we can create within ourselves and the more we stand to benefit from being in accord with and open to the positive energies that are available to us. This is the gift of the Air Element.

When this element is in need of rebalancing, a regime of yoga practice, martial arts, body building workouts, creative visualization techniques or meditation practices are beneficial.

> "See the light within which is free from all suffering and sorrow."
>
> ~ Pantanjali

Ether Element
Housed in the Vishuddi Chakra

"We must be willing to relinquish the life we've planned so as to have the life that is waiting for us."

~ Joseph Campbell

Location: The throat, neck, cervical plexus and brachial plexus

Function: Communication, hearing, creativity, charm

Sense: Hearing

Body parts: Thyroid, parathyroid, endocrine system, nerves, joints.

Qualities: Space, stillness, harmony, well-being, spiritual insights, and an integrated ego. Gentleness, true communication, integration, peace, creative expression.

Imbalances: Lack of creativity, grief, pride, ignorance, depression, thyroid problems, colds, communication problems, complaining, gossip.

An Ether-dominant person would find a satisfying home within the diplomatic service. This type of person is very tactful and skilled in the art of managing complicated communications.

Those who have a well-developed ether element are often gifted orators, like President Obama and Martin Luther King, singers and inspirational teachers. When this element is balanced, this type of individual is very appealing and quietly charming. They exhibit good rapport skills and may be drawn to work in storytelling, writing, public speaking, the media, mediation, high-level international relations, meditation, spirituality, music, singing, entertainment or spiritual practice all of which supports the balancing of this element.

However, when this element is imbalanced the person is often ungrounded, vacuous, uncommunicative and prone to gossip. To bring this element back into balance, it is helpful to engage with activities such as art and museum visits or to attend art, singing, music and meditation classes.

It is the Ether Element that gives us the quality of discrimination. Combined with Fire, it bestows upon us spiritual insights and an expanded awareness of boundaries and ethics. This element is nourished and amplified through meditation. Once the individual is strong in the lower chakras they will feel capable of speaking their truth clearly from this chakra. This element supports all the other elements and is considered the field within which everything exists.

The Yogal Portal

The Yogal Portal

The Postures

The Yogal Portal

Mountain Pose
Earth Element
and Ajna Chakra

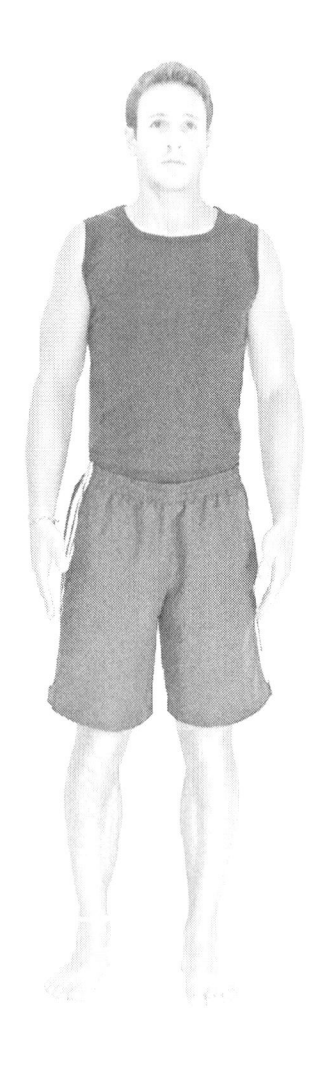

"When I let go of what I am, I become what I might be."
~ Lao Tzu

Mountain Pose
Earth Element
and Ajna Chakra

Mountain Pose invites us to move beyond the physical formation of the posture and to look instead in the direction toward which it points.

As we assume this pose, our focus is on the earth element. Gradually, we move our attention to the Ajna Chakra, the location of the third eye, which has no element attached to it but is the place where we can change our perspectives, clarify our perceptions and expand our inner landscape.

In our everyday lives, the awareness of our core qualities and natural states are usually overshadowed by the turbulence of our thoughts and the busyness of our daily lives. A personal practice or path that we can use regularly to create an alternate space is a good way to break the cycle of mechanical activity.

When we fully embody the Mountain Pose, our appreciation for the beauty and power to be found in nature is stimulated and we can see more clearly our part in it and understand more deeply the responsibility we all share towards our inheritance, the environment. It is then that we know ourselves to be truly wealthy, not in the sense of ownership but rather as custodians of a great legacy.

Lakshmi, Hindu Goddess of Good Fortune
courtesy of www.lotussculpture.com

The upward aspect of the Mountain Pose suggests a bringing together of heaven and earth. Like the Indian goddess Lakshmi, a Hindu symbol of wealth and prosperity, both material and spiritual, this posture captures the sense of balance we can experience when our feet are rooted in the earth and our heads in the clouds.

Mountain Pose conveys a sense of movement from a gross to a more refined nature, from the profane to the divine, from solid, material ground through to its polar opposite of connectedness with the universal cosmic consciousness.

The Yogal Portal

Dancer Pose
Nataraj's Dance
Fire Element and Ajna Chakra

"We shall not cease from exploration
And at the end of all our exploring
Will be to arrive where we started
And know the place for the first time."

~ T.S. Eliot

Dancer Pose
Nataraj's Dance
Fire Element and Ajna Chakra

The Dancer Pose represents the dance of life; the cosmic cycles of creation and destruction as well as the daily rhythm of birth and death. In this posture, we seek to free ourselves from our attachments and to find liberation through the dance of life. It is a distilling process requiring some skill.

Assuming the Dancer pose stimulates the Ajna (third eye) chakra and the fire element. This centre is also called the three rivers because this is where the Ida, Pingala and Sushumna nadis meet and terminate with Sushumna continuing its journey up to the crown chakra. As the Fire element makes its journey upwards, great spiritual insight, depth of concentration, the siddhis[5], gifts of perception, shifts in consciousness, all enter the realm of possibility. In working with the fire element and our Ajna intuition[6], we

---

[5] The acquisition of supernatural powers by psychic means or the supposed faculty so acquired.

[6] The sixth (Ajna) chakra or "third eye" is closely associated with imagination, inner vision and psychic abilities. It functions as a link between our inner and outer worlds.

can burn away our ignorance, shatter our illusions and ready ourselves for movement into emancipation and grace.

At the brow centre we find the Rudra Granthi, the last psychic or energetic knot which exerts some restraint in the process of transformation, giving the Ajna chakra the time it needs to become acclimated to the new energy.

The myth of Shiva Nataraj, King of the dancers, is paradoxical in that the posture conveys movement simultaneously with inner serenity or composure. In yoga there is more than one dancer posture, most likely because the discipline is keen to impart the wisdom inherent in this myth - that it is possible to experience stillness and to keep our composure even in the midst of motion.

This dance tells the story of our redemption as we move through the annihilation of our illusions, and seek to transcend our lack of knowledge to once again experience the creative force as it urges us towards another stage of life.

The Yogal Portal

Shiva Nataraj, King of the Dancers
courtesty of www.salagram.net

Triangle Pose
Trikonasana
Fire, Air and Ether Elements

"The most beautiful experience we can have is the mysterious.
It is the fundamental emotion which stands at the cradle of true art
and true science. Whoever does not know it and can no longer wonder,
no longer marvel, is as good as dead, and his eyes are dimmed."

~ Albert Einstein

Triangle Pose
Trikonasana
Fire, Air and Ether Elements

The triangle is highly utilized in the field of engineering because it forms a very powerful base, resisting pressure and providing a good support structure. In the practice of the Japanese martial art, Jiu Jitsu, the triangular locks are the most powerful.

The main elements stimulated by this asana are fire, air and ether. Athena, Greek goddess of wisdom, whose many attributes included courage, inspiration, civilization, law, justice, mathematics, strength, strategy, and the arts, as well as Nike, the winged goddess of victory, personify some of the varied aspects of the elements at work in this asana.

In the preparatory stage of this posture, as we stand with our legs astride and arms spread wide, we engage with the fiery currents of subtle energy which radiate out through the navel and across the body diagonally to the arms and legs.

From the fire chakra, our centre of empowerment, we open the chest and, travelling on the golden flames, we allow the fiery currents to move through the heart chakra to stimulate the air currents which rise up to the throat chakra creating a sense of spaciousness and giving the fire current the movement and expansion it needs to create warmth and healing throughout the body.

On a subtle energetic level there are many fascinating things in juxtaposition in Triangle pose. Just between the Manipura and Anahata chakras lies the second knot, Vishnu Granthi. To engage specifically with this granthi, in a separate practice, we can apply Uddiyana Bandha (abdominal lock), which encourages kundalini to rise through the Sushumna nadi. (See diagram on page 19).

In this pose, there is an upward and downward pointing triangle. The upward pointing triangle representing the masculine principle of fire, moving with expansion and ascending from the earthly to the heavenly realms. The downward pointing aspect of the triangle conveys the feminine principle of water, cohesion and divine grace, moving from the heavenly to the earthly realms.

The union of sun and moon, heaven and earth and the masculine and feminine principles, brings us the reward of a marriage of the opposites. This is the union of Shakti and Shiva, culminating in the ideal experience of oneness.

This asana affords us an opportunity to develop the strength we need to support ourselves and imbues us with a sense of empowerment. In this posture, we might ask ourselves:

Am I in right relationship with my will?

Am I giving myself the right kind of support?

Do I have a sense of grace surrounding me?

Trikonasana is itself a triad. There are three triangles within this posture which make it very potent and even moreso when we take into account the quality that certain numbers carry. Pythagoras, the Greek mathematician, proposed that odd numbers are masculine and even numbers, feminine. In Christianity, the number three represents the Blessed Trinity of God the Father, Son and Holy Spirit and the triad of body, mind and spirit. In Buddhism, its counterpart is the Triple Gem which comprises The Buddha (the highest spiritual potential within all human beings), The Dharma (the teachings of the Buddha) and the Sangha (the Buddhist community). In the Chinese culture, it communicates wholeness.

In perfecting this posture we are using our bodies to create a powerful archetype of integration and wholeness - attributes which, over time, we hope to make our own.

The Yogal Portal

Warrior Pose
Virabhadrasana
Earth and Fire Elements

"There is no chance, no destiny, no fate,
can circumvent or hinder or control
the firm resolve of a determined soul."

~ Ella Wilcox

Warrior Pose
Virabhadrasana
Earth and Fire Elements

When we practise the warrior posture we bring two elements to the fore, earth and fire. This strong martial posture makes good use of the stability which the earth offers to the warrior. Interestingly, this pose forms a square shape in the lines running between the feet and from fingertips to feet. There is also a rectangular shape between the legs. Squares and rectangles are shapes that express the strength, stability, steadiness and integrity of the earth. Not only is the posture stimulating the earth element, but the body's shape, in a very elegant interplay of symbols, also holds within it the symbol of the earth.

As we move into the posture, we can feel the base chakra being stimulated as we bend the knee and lower the hips. One of the negative aspects that is sometimes encountered in the earth element is fearfulness. Unless we recognize this trait and work towards transforming it, we may become trapped. We need to understand that courage is not merely the absence of fear, it is rather an acknowledgement of fear and a deliberate engagement with the challenges that we face. The fear serves to inform us of the dangers of the situation and courage prevents us from walking away.

The fire element, once kindled, will convey its focus and drive, forging a pathway for courage to emerge as we work towards bringing these two elements into harmony.

In the allegory of the Bhagavad Gita, Arjuna the warrior prince is instructed by his guide, Lord Krishna on different states of consciousness, reality, meditation practice, the way of love and the path to freedom. As Arjuna faces 'the war within', he says to Krishna:

> 'life goes from my limbs, my mouth is dry, a trembling overcomes my body.'

Krishna's advice is:

> 'Neither agitated by grief nor hankering after pleasure, they live free from fear and anger. Established in meditation they are truly wise.'

In other words, despair in a time of crisis brings you no merit.

In the 'Gita', yoga refers to the skill of union with the ultimate reality or the Absolute. The stance of the Warrior Pose can empower and stimulate our consciousness to bring forth the qualities of determination and focus for transformation.

The Goddess Durga, whose name means a fort or place which is difficult to overrun, is a fierce, multi-armed warrior deity from Indian Mythology who is the female representation of the energy of creation and destruction and a good example of the combination of the earth and fire elements.

Durga, Goddess of Victory of Good over Evil

Durga is called forth when order needs to be re-established and everything else has failed. She is portrayed riding a lion, conveying her enormous power and skill in conquering the physical, mental and spiritual obstacles that can materialize when the earth and fire elements are opposed.

When these elements come into balance, we find the strength and courage to do whatever we need to, even if it is unpleasant, in order to uphold our sense of integrity.

The Yogal Portal

Tree Pose
Vrkasana
Ether Element and Ajna Chakra

"My material body and the body of the Universe both flicker in and out of existence at the speed of light."

~ Deepak Chopra

Tree Pose
Vrkasana
Ether Element and Ajna Chakra

The chakras stimulated in the Tree pose are Ajna and Vishuddhi. Ajna means to know, to perceive. Vishuddhi means to purify. Ajna is associated with the third eye and has no element. Vishuddhi's element is ether.

There is a belief in Hinduism that when something is seen in the mind's eye or in a dream, it is being 'seen' by Ajna and that Ajna is an intuitive bridge that allows mind communication to occur between people.

In the Tree pose one can experience a sense of balance. Balance of mind, emotions and body. As we assume the shape of a tree, we feel ourselves connecting with our roots which extend deep into the earth giving us support and balance as we stand on one leg. The Ether element lends a quality of spaciousness and deepens our sense of equilibrium.

When we move further into the pose and lift our arms upwards, we become conscious of our connection with the heavens and are aware that we are working with gravity to be rooted in the earth and simultaneously against it to reach skyward in an attempt to reconcile these two polarities.

Whether it is a good or bad day when we come to our mats, we can use Tree Pose to bring us to a calm centre. When we approach this posture with Intention, Attention and Awareness it becomes obvious that, should we lose our attention, very soon we will be unable to hold the pose. Attention is key as we are constantly adjusting and readjusting the balance throughout the pose until we come into the zone and can rest in this position. This right effort (intention) in the application of the posture enhances the quality of our Awareness and fills us with a sense of spacious calm and expanded peacefulness.

When the Ajna chakra is stimulated and the breath continues to move through the subtle energy system, if we are sufficiently grounded and allow ourselves to be open to 'heavenly' or ether-influenced energies, we may find that our perceptions change regarding our issues and that certain questions arise in our minds such as:

"Am I able to maintain my balance while I open to this experience?"

"In the midst of the difficulties and challenges of life can I still hold that sense of equilibrium?"

Like the trees and plants, we learn to bend and sway. Staying flexible, we neither push nor pull but adapt to circumstances when our internal weather comes up. Staying present in the moment, we are better able to make mindful choices and avoid being drawn into excess.

Have you ever walked in a forest or tended trees and had the feeling that they would speak to you if they could? And that the rustling of their leaves was simply a message you could not translate?

Looked at symbolically, trees represent ourselves with their cycles of growth, death and rebirth. In the language of dreams, a tree generally symbolizes spiritual, intellectual or emotional growth. The Buddha experienced enlightenment while sitting under the Bodhi Tree, a sacred fig tree in Indian mythology which even today is still sought out as a sacred exemplary centre.

The shape of a tree denotes a sharing of energies through its many branches. When it blossoms and bears fruit its sharing then extends beyond itself because the produce is not required for its own sustenance. This sharing profoundly communicates to us that we are in relationship to everything in nature and the understanding of this concept elicits our highest perspectives as we continue to evolve. This insight is the gift of Tree pose.

Eagle Pose
Garudasana
Earth Element

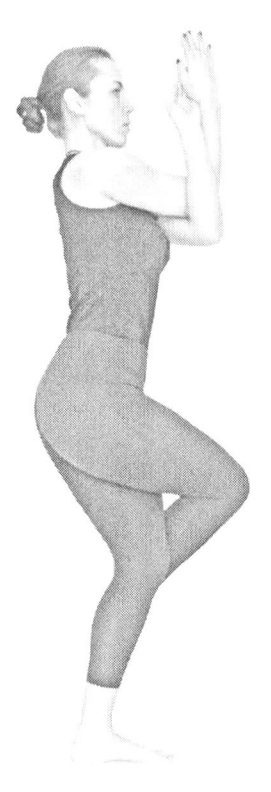

"The most important characteristic of the Eastern world view
– one could almost say the essence of it –
is the awareness of the unity and mutual interrelation
of all things and events, the experience of all phenomena
in the world as manifestations of a basic oneness.
All things are seen as interdependent
and inseparable parts of this cosmic whole;
as different manifestations of the same ultimate reality."

~ Fritjof Capra

Eagle Pose
Garudasana
Earth Element

*"Peace, and be at peace with your thoughts and visions.
These things had to come to you and you to accept them.
This is your share of the eternal burden.
The perpetual glory. This is one moment,
but know that another shall pierce you
with a sudden painful joy."*

~ T.S. Eliot

This posture represents the mythical creature Garuda, King of Birds, found in texts of a major branch of Hinduism called Vaishnavism. He is resplendent in his beauty with the body of a man and the head, wings, talons and back of an eagle. During his life he was set many challenges and obstacles to overcome. He had a strong dislike of evil and displayed great courage and bravery in overcoming his difficulties.

As we come into this posture the wrapping of the limbs around each other forms a spiral shape which proclaims original, ingenious and creative thinking. The shape mimics the double helix of our DNA which looks like and is sometimes referred to as a spiralling staircase. It is suggestive of speed, directness and the rising and descending of energy. This graceful shape directs energy through our bodies, silently exerting its influence on our minds, bodies and spirits as it subtly deepens our experience of the Eagle Pose.

Through this asana, the opportunity of working with the base chakra arises. The Mooladahara chakra is governed by the earth element whose gift to us is courage. When the energies of the base chakra are stimulated, we develop grounding, stability and encouragement to move beyond fear and anxiety.

Garuda, King of Birds
courtesy of www.dharmakshetra.com

Moving through the subtle levels and deeper into this posture, we embrace the positive qualities of bravery and wisdom that the eagle imparts which helps us to gain a wider, more 'eagle-eyed' perspective from our now loftier perch.

Obtaining the strength and courage that this pose inspires does not happen overnight and like the patient, mythological Greek god of agriculture, Triptolemus, who was taught many farming ideas and techniques by Demeter, the mother of the earth, which he, in turn, painstakingly taught others, we must be tolerant with ourselves while we develop what is needed in order to cultivate skill and share the knowledge. And, we must commit to practise, practise, practise, if we desire to be competent at anything.

The image of an eagle, whether in dreams or reality, encourages us to reach beyond our usual limits and to strive for excellence with patience and resolve. Its message is to let our spirits soar and thus increase our wisdom by virtue of the higher perspective gained through having a better view of the landscape. It does not ask for mercy or for gifts but rather makes good use of that which is inherent in its structure and nature.

Native American Indians see the eagle as a symbol of leadership and vision and many countries use it as a symbol of hope and dominion. The archetype of the eagle connotes an association with the heavens yet remains strongly connected to the earth for even as it makes its home as close to the sky as it can, it also finds its sustenance on the ground.

This powerful image offers us the gift of uniting new vision with successful, astute outcomes.

The Yogal Portal

Shiva's Dance Pose
Natarajasana
Ajna chakra

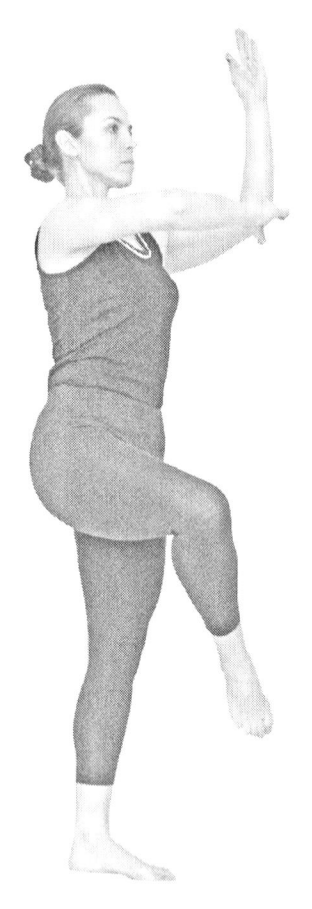

"The way of the Creative works through change
and transformation, so that each thing
receives its true nature and destiny
and comes into permanent accord with the Great Harmony,
this is what furthers and preserves."

~ Alexander Pope

Shiva's Dance Pose
Natarajasana
Ajna Chakra

Shiva is a primary Hindu deity known by many names, the most ubiquitous of which are "The Destroyer" and "The Transformer". At first glance, we might think that those names are mutually exclusive and have nothing in common until we realize that in order for something to be transformed, its original form must essentially be destroyed.

Shiva's Dance is a dance of creation and liberation. His image usually depicts him encircled by a ring of fire which represents not only the universe itself but the constant flow of energy between him and the cosmos as well as the perpetual cycle of death and rebirth; all powerfully illustrating the union between the spiritual and the physical.

This image very eloquently expresses our interdependence and interrelatedness with the universe. We are not as separate from each other as we like to believe and are intimately connected to the universe even though our levels of awareness may sometimes lead us to think otherwise.

Most images of Shiva portray him with an animal,

usually underfoot, signifying his karma; his actions which he has overcome but to which he remains connected, conveying the message of liberation over delusion.

Shiva, Lord of the Cosmic Dance

The shape of Shiva's posture is one of fluid, circular movement. The curves of his body represent activity, drive and rhythm. The circle in which he stands is a universal symbol of wholeness and infinity, often used to represent Ultimate Unity and/or Reality. Shiva's position in the centre asserts that we are included in this divine 'dance' process. These symbols form part of our global culture and while Shiva's Cosmic Dance may convey a multitude of meanings, it also carries an unequivocal message of universal timelessness.

In this posture, the Ajna chakra is stimulated. Ajna, which means to command or to know, is often referred to as the third eye or perception centre. It is largely concerned with knowledge and intuition. This chakra is not attached to an element but is a point where the Ida, Pingala and Sushumna meridians converge. Once the Ajna is awakened, our powers of perception become enhanced, new perspectives ensue and we feel liberated from our old ways of viewing the world and ourselves. Shiva represents the process of change which also embodies the concept of letting go. In our practise of yoga and meditation and of Shiva's Dance pose in particular, we can allow the energies stimulated by this posture to transform our false identification with form and surrender to the process of change. As we come out on the other side, letting go of restricting habits and old attachments, we open to the beauty of new beginnings, changing viewpoints and new insights.

Standing in this posture, we evoke the spirit of Shiva, Lord of the Cosmic Dance who symbolizes victory over vice and the establishment of divine order. Practising this posture helps us to maintain our equilibrium as the Ajna chakra awakens and shatters old delusions leaving us better equipped to face life with a renewed sense of physical and emotional balance and poise.

The Yogal Portal

Gate Pose
Parighasana
Earth and Water Elements

"Our pains announce deficiencies, excesses, breakages, displacements,
shifting balances within the complexities of our organic lives,
and often in order to resolve them we have to learn something about
these complicated internal affairs of ours...
For this experience of self-examination and revelation,
we require situations which the experts cannot resolve,
situations which throw us back onto our own resources.
This is how we learn that we have resources."

~ Deane Juhan, author of Job's body

Gate Pose
Parighasana
Earth and Water Elements

"The difference between stumbling blocks and stepping stones is how you use them."

~ Unknown

Looking at our physical bodies holistically and taking into account the parts we can and cannot see, it is not difficult to imagine the body as a first line of defence or as a bar used to secure a gate. A gate implies that there is something of value in need of protection or a threshold through which you can, if you have the key, gain access to the treasure within.

In this posture two shapes emerge, that of the crescent moon or half circle as well as a small triangle. A crescent moon may either be in the waxing or waning phase. The waxing moon represents a potential for growth, increase or completion of an accomplishment while the waning moon implies a time or attitude of yielding; a relinquishing and letting go of outmoded, useless ideas, opinions or positions. Then we have the triangle which, among many other things, stands for the trinity of truth, love and wisdom. The richness of the symbology of this posture can provide much impetus for transformation.

In the practise of Gate Pose, the earth and water elements are stimulated encouraging the rise of the dormant, vital energy, also referred to as Kundalini. When these elements are balanced, they convey a sense of security enabling us to meet the difficulties of life with fortitude and equanimity. This allows us to shift from the subjective experience of being overly concerned with ourselves and focus on the larger, objective world as the stimulation of these elements facilitates our understanding of the concept 'contributing to the benefit of all'.

At this earth-water junction lies the first psychic knot, Brahma granthi; a psychic or energetic knot which slows down or inhibits the free flow of prana being transmuted along the sushmuna nadi or channel. Only if sufficient prior psychological and soul work has taken place will this energy be free to rise and descend, thereby rebalancing itself.

An important question to ask ourselves as we prepare to work with these two elements is:

> "Am I sufficiently grounded to face the new world that will open to me as I pass through this portal?"

Earth and Water Elements, when imbalanced and manifesting negatively, have a propensity to express themselves in depression and a feeling that we are carrying the world on our shoulders; our emotional lives become heavy weather. Often you'll hear someone who is experiencing this Earth/Water imbalance opine that other people lead such charmed lives and that the burdens weren't shared out equally.

The Earth and Water elements govern and manage the musculoskeletal system. This system protects our vital organs and allows us freedom of movement. It is the job of our internal organs to get sufficient blood and nutrients to the musculoskeletal system to keep it in good working order and the skeletal system is, in turn, responsible for giving birth to the new red blood cells in the bone marrow. Through our practice of yoga, we can do our part to keep the system refreshed and working optimally.

Worldly pleasures, the routines and stresses of everyday life, all work towards maintaining our external focus. However, the Yoga model is interested in progression beyond the ego. According to Patanjali, the great sage who wrote the Yoga Sutras, there are five obstacles that prevent the expansion of spiritual growth and they are:

1. Ignorance (Avidya)
2. Egoism (Asmita)
3. Cravings (Raga)
4. Aversions (Dwesha)
5. Clinging to life (Abhinivesha)

These obstacles are a veritable bag of gold and like everything else in life, if we want to be good at something we have to apply effort and engagement because it is through working with 'our stuff' and letting go of our anger, jealousy, ignorance, hatred and cravings that we create the space for spiritual growth and expansion.

The Yogal Portal

Downward Facing Dog
Adho Mukha Svanasana
Ether Element and Crown Chakra

"If peacefulness is our aim, renunciation must be our path – of this we have no choice. Emptying the heart and mind of desires,
of our self-image, of expectations, of being somebody special
and instead filling it with generosity will open the door to loving-kindness.
Until we actually make that happen, loving-kindness remains a hope and an unfulfilled expectation."

~ Ayya Khema

Downward Facing Dog
Adho Mukha Svanasana
Ether Element and Crown Chakra

This posture works very powerfully to stimulate the spinal nerves and muscles, boosting the circulation of prana throughout the body, while offering alignment to the spinal column, especially the upper back. This posture creates a concert of energy flow between the chakras, culminating in the Vishuddi and Crown chakras forming a very strong triangular, pyramid shape. We can readily see how it supports pressure and tension. Correspondingly, this upward pointing triangle which represents the masculine principle of drive, progression and intention evokes an appreciation of the beautiful alchemy created by the interface of posture, with its inherent meaning and myth, and the subtle energy system.

This merging of energies through the Sushumna nadi enjoys the spacious stillness and the purifying process of the Ether element as it prepares for ascendancy to and attainment of the Crown chakra. This chakra, which does not have an element attached, has to do with the development of wisdom, a compassionate mind and loving-kindness. This is the place of self-transcendence and insightful awareness.

When we release the hooks of our self-centredness which drives our pain then the envy, anger, addictions, hatred and fear are all transformed and we find ourselves on a more peaceful path. In Buddhist tradition, these obstacles give rise to our sense of dukkha, a Sanskrit word which is often translated as 'suffering' although it does not do justice to the concept which is multilayered and includes the physical, mental and emotional pains we experience. It also refers to our dissatisfaction with the transitory nature of life and to the unease we feel that things will not live up to our expectations.

Through gentle and steady progression in our yoga and meditation practice, we embrace the experiences of heightened awareness, broadened perspectives and altered states of consciousness as we move in the direction of the ultimate peak experience of unity consciousness.

An awakening and liberation from an ego-bound perspective is an experience available to anyone who cares to develop awareness and insight. When we find this experience elusive, it is usually because we allow ourselves to be distracted by the external world. In a society where there is a plethora of information available on the subject of spiritual paths and a multitude of teachers, it remains our choice whether or not to engage our consciousness on a path of transcendence.

The Yogal Portal

"To have humility is to experience reality,
not in relation to ourselves,
but in its sacred independence.
It is to see, judge, and act
from the point of rest in ourselves.
Then, how much disappears,
and all that remains falls into place..."

~ Dag Hammarskjöld

Cobra Pose
Bhujangasana
Water Element and Crown Chakra

"Of how it is that the soul informs the body,
physical science teaches me nothing and that living matter influences
and is influenced by mind is a mystery without a clue.
Consciousness is not explained to my comprehension by all the nerve
paths and neurons of the physiologist,
nor do I ask physics how goodness shines in one man's face
and evil betrays itself in another."

~ D'Arcy Thompson

Cobra Pose
Bhujangasana
Water Element and Crown Chakra

The cobra regularly sheds its skin, recreating itself in much the same way we do as seekers on the way to becoming more fully ourselves. The cobra represents wisdom, expectant watchfulness, rebirth, renewal and sexual energy.

In this posture, the main chakras stimulated are the Swadhisthana Chakra which houses both the Water element that we cultivate and express by learning to move effortlessly into, out of and between postures, and the Crown Chakra at the top of the head whose inner aspect deals with the release of karma.

The Swadhisthana Chakra is associated with unconscious desires especially those of a sexual nature and is where the various potential karmas lie dormant. It is said that to raise the energy of consciousness above Swadhisthana is extremely difficult for this reason. Throughout the ages many saints have had to face sexual temptations associated with this chakra whose key issues are relationships, addictions, basic emotional needs and pleasure.

As the Water element stimulates the Fire centre, the fire element imparts its light and direction, driving the prana upwards. The chest is open, allowing the air element to share its quality of effortless movement as the majesty of this amalgam moves along the spine up to the Crown centre in the arising of wisdom. As the crown centre unfolds and evolves over time, we may progress towards gradual experiences of altered states of consciousness and brief glimpses of unity consciousness which gives rise to a sense of bliss.

The Cobra poses the questions:

"How open am I to transformation?"

"Can I observe the old habits and attitudes that still cling on, creating obstacles?"

"How do I deal with the mini deaths and rebirths occurring in my life?"

"Can I watch with wisdom, the poisons of my mind?"

"Can I arise from this renewed?"

"As I approach this asana, am I ready for the creative experience of liberation?"

This posture makes us aware of the responsibilities that come with the arising of the wisdom we hope to achieve when practising this shape. Once we have seen the light we cannot return to the dark; our minds cannot shrink once they've expanded, and therein lies the rub.

Saraswati, daughter of Lord Shiva and the Goddess Durga, very adequately portrays the integration of these energies. She is depicted as a beautiful woman representing harmony, cosmic knowledge, intelligence, enlightenment, education and the arts. She is admired not only because she is erudite but also because she has experience of the highest reality. Imagine for a moment, what those attributes might look like in reality - to have beauty that is not only skin deep but augmented by wisdom, intellect and clarity of purpose, clothed in a personality imbued with harmony and unconditional love. She is, indeed, the ultimate role model.

The Crown centre, located at the top of the head does not have an element associated with it but functions as a channel connecting us to divine consciousness, insight and wisdom. This is our seat of liberation and transcendence. As our awareness grows and the Crown chakra becomes vibrant and established, we begin to see past the ego and our perspectives and lives are forever changed. Our false view of separateness falls away and we are beside ourselves with rapture and unconditional love for others, yet we remain unable to adequately define or express the experience.

This expanded sense[7] of self is based on a clear awareness of the interconnected fabric of life of which we are a part and which sustains us. When awakened to the reality of our relatedness to all of Life, we can overcome the fear of change and experience the deeper continuities beyond and beneath the ceaseless flow of change.

It is a great challenge to attend to our spiritual practice in the midst of our everyday lives yet we all have the potential to access and experience a Unified or Bliss Consciousness within ourselves. Working with the Water and Crown chakras prepares us for the profound insights that are ultimately the result of our efforts.

Saraswati
www.salagram.net

---

[7] Courtesy of Soka Gakkai International

The Yogal Portal

"Our birth is but a sleep and a forgetting:
The soul that rises with us, our life's star,
Hath had elsewhere its setting,
And cometh from afar:
Not in entire forgetfulness,
And not in utter nakedness,
But trailing clouds of glory do we come."

~ Wordsworth

Hero's Pose
Veersasana
Ajna Chakra

"Furthermore, we have not even to risk the adventure alone, for the heroes of all time have gone before us. The labyrinth is thoroughly known. We have only to follow the thread of the hero path, and where we had thought to find an abomination, we shall find a god. And where we had thought to slay another we shall slay ourselves. Where we had thought to travel outward, we will come to the centre of our own existence. And where we had thought to be alone, we shall be with all the world."

~ Joseph Campbell

Hero's Pose
Veersasana
Ajna Chakra

The definition of a hero or heroine is a man or woman who commits an act of tremendous bravery, sometimes from a position of weakness. Classical mythology and storytelling throughout the ages abound with them.

The ancient Greek poet Homer, in his famous work the Iliad, gave us Achilles, hero of the Trojan War who demonstrated outstanding bravery. The Bhagavad Gita's epic story of the power of non-attachment illustrated through the dialogues between Arjuna, an Indian warrior Prince known for his skill in archery and his Lord Krishna, who advised him on what he considered to be the most important war - the war within - show two very different types of hero, each bringing forth some remarkable characteristic in overcoming the obstacles and hurdles with which they were confronted.

When we sit in Hero's pose we are invited to focus our attention on the Ajna Chakra, considered the eye of intuition. When something is seen through the mind's eye, it comes via this chakra and it is here that we can access our own inner Arjuna.

This asana can be used to stimulate our powers of intuition when we encounter obstacles and difficulties in our lives and to elicit the necessary strength or bravery to defeat them. In so doing, we come to know our capabilities and power. This posture is also a good practice for those who would like to develop their concentration.

When the energies of this chakra are stimulated and the brow centre opens, it offers gifts of extraordinary perception and knowledge bypassing the ordinary sense of knowing. This is the junction where Sushumna, Ida and Pingala coalesce. However, the masculine and feminine principles of energy terminate here and only Sushumna continues its journey to the Crown chakra. Although the word Sushumna cannot be adequately translated into English, it signifies the state of an undisturbed and joyous mind.

At this brow chakra lies the third and last psychic knot, the Rudra Granthi. The Granthis can be likened to a filter which allows the chakras to become established in the new frequency of energy flow that results after they have been worked with. These knots slow down the free movement of prana being transmuted along the Sushumna nadi so that transformation is gradual and changes comfortably assimilated.

When we incorporate Jalandhara Bandha which is more commonly known as the Chin Bandha, into our practice, we directly engage with the Rudra Granthi which will redirect the prana to flow through Sushumna, piercing the Granthi and allowing Kundalini to rise.

There is no way to gain access past this Granthi or knot other than working with our issues. This journey requires courage and bravery if our demons are to be overcome. It is a Hero's journey and our reward lies in an expansion of consciousness where all sense of duality falls away, making it possible to experience an enhanced state of unity as our perceptions widen and we finally understand what is meant by the expressions "The dancer and the dance became one." or "Time stood still."

Boat Pose
Paripurna Navasana
Swadhisthana & Manipura Chakras

"If you follow your bliss, you put yourself on a kind
of track that has been there all the while, waiting for you,
and the life that you ought to be living is the one you are living. Wherever
you are, if you are following your bliss,
you are enjoying that refreshment, that life within you, all the time."

~ Joseph Campbell

Boat Pose
Paripurna Navasana
Swadhisthana & Manipura Chakras

Even as we perform boat pose, the deeper significance of this shape reveals itself to us. In mythology, the boat often represents destiny and our journey through life. In ancient times, the boat had been seen as a vessel used to move souls of the dead to the afterlife. The biblical story of Noah and his ark illustrates this well by presenting the image of a vessel that maintains stability as it moves through troubled waters and transports us to new beginnings. Armed with this image of transportation and movement, we create the relevant mind-set needed to deal with our emotions as we undertake the work of transforming ourselves.

Both the water and fire elements are stimulated by the boat pose. Besides its association with birth, the water element has a deeply spiritual nature. In dream symbology, our individual psyches are often represented by small pools of water and the collective unconscious by larger bodies of water. We often talk of being washed clean and the cleansing practises of yoga and ayurveda which are physical rituals that are meant to imply an internal or spiritual purification are a pertinent example of this.

The observation in nature of sunlight on water which

creates the effect of a reflective mirror, makes it easier for us to imagine the positive unification of the fire and water energies in ourselves, which may, over time, give us the experience of deep, personal insights as we contemplate the meaning of that which is reflected back to us.

When there is an imbalance in the combination of water and fire elements, we experience turbulent emotions and stormy, unpredictable, internal weather. Water always seeks its lowest level and fire speaks to light and consciousness. Consequently, if we work mindfully and intentionally with these two elements there will inevitably arise opportunities through the water element to make ourselves aware of any issues which are, as yet, unconscious within us and with the aid of the fire element, what has been dark and unknown to us will be brought up for healing through the firelight of our understanding.

As we work towards balancing the two elements, a quality of expansion and radiance is created as they transform and influence each other, culminating in a sense of vitality and wellbeing; the fire giving direction and boundary as the water energy rises to seek its new level. Water, as a symbol of unconscious energy, also relates to our emotions, many of which are driven by unconscious forces until the fire of our intelligence shines its light onto the muddy waters and brings forth clarity.

Twist of a Sage
Ardha Matsyendrasana
Water and Fire Elements

"Everybody wants to be somebody who has certain attributes, views, opinions and ideas, even if it is only Don Quixote tilting against windmills. We even hold on to patently wrong views because they make the "I" more solid.
We may think it is negative and depressing to be nobody and have nothing, but... as we may find out for ourselves, it is the most exhilarating and liberating feeling we can ever have. But because we fear that the windmills might attack us, we do not let go of our illusions."

~ Ayya Khema

Twist of a Sage
Ardha Matsyendrasana
Water and Fire Elements

In the Yoga system, the seven main chakras or energy centres lie along the spine. This posture stimulates these centres creating movement up and down the energy fields, the long line currents and meridian lines that run the length of the body. The spiral shape present in the posture is indicative of the movement of energy and also communicates the idea of flexibility.

When this movement of energy also effects a change in our consciousness as the shape speaks to us on a non-verbal level, we come to realize the potential of the postures to profoundly nourish and transform us.

The negative aspects of a knot or twist are those of limitation and imprisonment. For example, we are tied to the wheel of life by the positions and beliefs we adhere to and unless we are prepared to relinquish these positions (or knots), we are unable to free ourselves. A lot of energy is invested in the creation and maintenance of our viewpoints and opinions, yet these are the very things that keep us from experiencing the intimacy and freedom that we need and long for in our lives.

The positive aspect of a knot is that of integration and liberty. When we allow ourselves to let go of those positions that limit us, freedom can be our windfall.

The area that experiences the most twist in this posture is the Manipura Chakra or the Fire Centre and when this element is stimulated we feel bright, clear and vital. This posture is not just about keeping our bodies pliant and supple, its subliminal message is also useful in bringing a measure of flexibility to our thinking, attitudes and minds. This asana induces us to release our excess baggage and defensive short-sightedness.

If our yoga is self-reflective, then it follows that we will take the insights acquired off the mat and into our lives which can have a very cathartic effect on our thinking, speech and relationships.

The Twist presents us with the opportunity to ask ourselves the following questions:

> "Am I flexible enough in my views or is my spine reflecting rigidity? Is the stiffness some idea that needs re-examining?"

> "Am I too flexible? Do I allow myself to be easily manipulated by others?"

> "Am I ready to take this chance to look at my attachments and explore a new insight?"

In Tibetan Buddhism, apart from conveying the Buddha's wisdom, the endless knot is a favourite symbol representing the interconnectedness of all events, past, present and future, through a cycle of cause and effect.

This endless knot is similar to the Celtic knot and these two have become very popular universal symbols for eternal life and the constant cycle of nature.

In Maori myth, the many twists of this symbol denote the bond between people through love, friendship or family ties. Its eternal inference represents the path of life.

The Buddhist Eternal Knot

ND
Bridge Pose
Setu Bandhasana
Fire, Air and Ether Elements

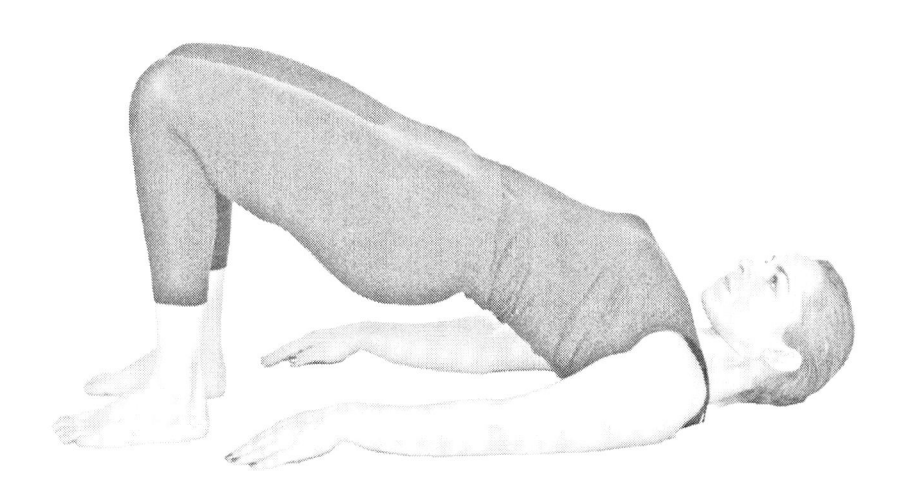

"Our bodies are our gardens, to which our wills
are gardeners; so that if we will plant nettles,
and sow lettuce, set hyssop and weed up thyme,
supply it with one gender of herbs or distract it
with many, either have it sterile with idleness
or manured with industry,
why, the power and corrigible authority
of this lies in our wills."

~ William Shakespeare, Othello

Bridge Pose
Setu Bandhasana
Fire, Air and Ether Elements

A Bridge is a means of transition; a structure which facilitates movement from one place or point to another. Implied within its organization is the idea of connectedness. In the language of dreams, it could signify a move between the unconscious and the conscious minds as we attempt to bring some hidden part of ourselves into the light in an effort to become more of who we really are. It also represents a point of connection between disparate ideas or people. This is part of the hero's journey and there are many bridges to cross.

This posture stimulates the Fire, Air and Ether elements. Ether provides the space for Fire to combine with Air. As the Air element communicates its ideals to the Fire element, it stimulates new thinking and in turn Fire shares its warmth with the Air element and opens its heart/hearth. This combination fosters good judgement, philosophical thinking, an appreciation for and enjoyment of learning, reading and the process of thinking.

The positive outcome of this blend of the Elements, sees Fire and Air being purified by Ether, while they in turn impart some of their unique qualities to Ether. Changes in the content of our thoughts take place as we reap the benefit of this purification and find ourselves making better decisions and judgements, and even communicating more clearly. This change creates a more harmonious mental environment within which our thinking is further distilled and our minds more receptive to new information.

Iris was chosen by the Greek gods to be the mediator and messenger between themselves and the people because she 'moved with the speed of the wind' between earth and the sky. Myth also ties her to the rainbow which the Greeks regarded as a bridge in the sky. When the Fire, Air and Ether elements are stimulated, they create a colourful rainbow which moves through the chakras along the spine, carrying and delivering its sacred message 'with the speed of the wind.'

When there is an imbalance in this combination there can be an excess of agitation, movement and overwork without adequate rest leading to collapse and burn out.

Working with the elements can help us to see ourselves and others more clearly. It can bring us to a deeper understanding of how we can become instrumental in balancing these energies, create more harmony in ourselves and each other and learn to build our own bridges of communication.

"A human being is part of the whole called by us 'universe', a part limited in time and space. We experience ourselves, our thoughts and feelings as something separate from the rest. A kind of optical delusion of consciousness. This delusion is a kind of prison for us, restricting us to our personal desires and to affection for a few persons nearest to us. Our task must be to free ourselves from the prison by widening our circle of compassion to embrace all living creatures and the whole of nature in its beauty. The true value of a human being is determined by the measure and the sense in which they have obtained liberation from the self [ego]. We shall require a substantially new manner of thinking if humanity is to survive."

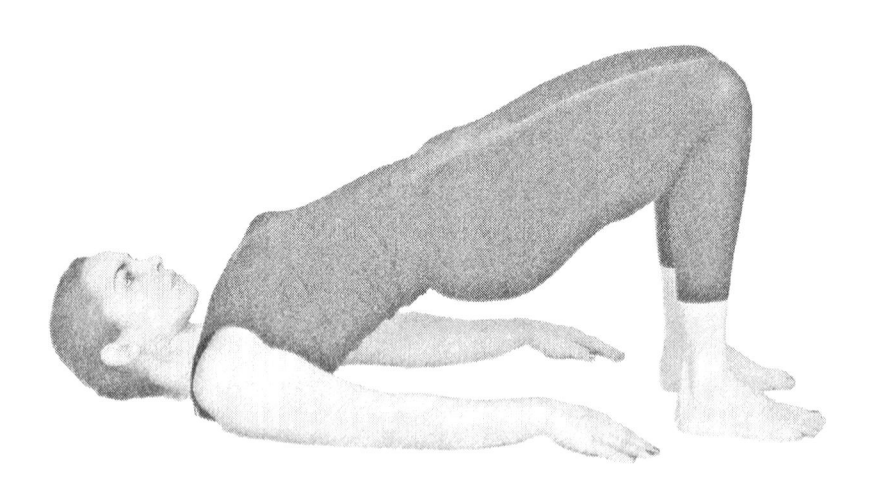

~ Albert Einstein

The Yogal Portal

Bow Pose
Dhanurasana
Air, Fire and Ether Elements

"The fruit of the spirit is love, joy, peace, patience, kindness, goodness, faithfulness, gentleness and self-control."

~ Galatians 5.22/23

Bow Pose
Dhanurasana
Air, Fire and Ether Elements

In bow posture, the Ether element housed in the throat chakra, the Air element in the heart chakra and the Fire element in the solar plexus chakra, are all quickened. The spine, through which the Ida, Pingala and Sushumna nadis reside, is given an intense stretch which realigns their energies. The circle implied in this posture offers us wholeness, integration, a sense of completion and beckons us to share in its gifts, not the least of which are evolution and greater insight.

In Native American Indian symbology, the bow and arrow convey direction, force and power. In ancient Roman times it denoted not only physical strength but the psychological fortitude needed to maintain government so, if we wanted to strengthen our sense of leadership, we might purposefully practise the Bow pose with the intent that this powerful posture will fortify our ability to manage ourselves.

The configuration of this posture blends the masculine and feminine energies; Ida being the feminine principle and Pingala, the masculine. Once the direction and force of these energies are engaged, the polarities unite and a marriage of opposites ensues.

Placing ourselves in this strong shape stimulates Kundalini to move through the spinal column and rise through the Sushumna nadi. In this most powerful of yoga back-bends, the confluence of energies which supports the arising of Kundalini continues as the arrows of the fire element rise. Momentum is gained and the *arrows* are propelled upwards to seek purification by the Ether element. This propulsion declares the possibility of the *arrows* travelling some distance, even beyond the Throat Chakra and, once again, our lowly yoga mat turns into a place of awakening.

The Buddha taught that everything we need for our experience of liberation is found in the body/mind phenomena, and Nichiren Buddhism[8] in particular, teaches that it is impossible to live in the world without attachments or indeed, to eradicate them. Our affections for others, the desire to succeed in our endeavours, our interests and passions, our love of life itself - all of these are attachments and potential sources of disappointment or suffering yet they are the substance of our humanity and elements of engaged and fulfilled lives.

According to this doctrine, the challenge is not to rid oneself of these attachments and desires but rather to

---

[8] Courtesy of Soka Gakkai International, www.sgi.org

become enlightened concerning them. When we can see them clearly and master them, we are truly liberated and free to lead interesting and significant lives.

Meditation

"The restless violence of the senses impetuously carries away
the mind of even a wise man striving towards perfection.....
But the soul that moves in the world of the senses and yet keeps the
senses in harmony, free from attraction and aversion,
finds rest in quietness.
In this quietness falls down the burden of all sorrows, for when
the heart has found quietness, wisdom has also found peace."

~ Bhagavad Gita

Meditation

As early as 1500 B.C., meditation is mentioned in the written records of the Hindu traditions of ancient India. Around the 6th to 5th centuries B.C., other forms of meditation developed in Taoist China and Buddhist India.

Meditation is central to Buddhism and is one of the eight limbs of the Yogic tradition. The East has a rich tradition of meditation while the West enjoys a historically shorter and less robust practice. In the West, our mode of understanding ourselves is primarily sought through psychotherapy although in recent decades huge strides have been made in the United Kingdom as well as in North America to incorporate a meditative framework into the psychotherapy treatment model.

By definition, meditation is not a therapy but aspects of it can be used as such. It is also not relaxation. It really is the hardest and most intimate work one can undertake in the pursuit of personal transformation and there are many different types to choose from: Zen, Mindfulness, Tibetan, Vipassana, Movement, Transcendental, Walking, Mantra, Qi Gong, Kum Nye and many others.

Meditation is the practice of focusing attention on an object, e.g., the breath, a candle flame, a sound or the repetition of a mantra, etc., in order to develop more awareness of yourself and Ultimate Reality. Through this cultivation of mindfulness (in Buddhism), awareness is expanded and the growth of our consciousness is stimulated. The distance between subject and object narrows and a new intimacy is born as we experience unity consciousness. It is a long road and one without a particular destination.

As seasoned meditators tell us, the gradual insights gained keep us returning to the path with the intention of steadily decreasing the distance between subject and object until we have what is referred to as a peak experience where we feel a deep sense of unity with all things as expressed in many of the Christian religions as "I and the Father are one." Or during sex, when we lose our feeling of separateness and "I and the beloved are one." When we witness a really great artiste or musician deliver a performance that brings everyone to their feet, we can easily identify almost exactly, the transformational moment when the dancer becomes the dance or the singer the song. Through meditation, it is possible for every person to experience their own Satchitananda - absolute bliss through the clarity of consciousness within their being.

While posture work, breathing techniques, karma yoga and other yoga practices are very significant and far-reaching in their ability to move us beyond our various forms of mental rigidity and stances, it is meditation that is the key to unlocking the core process.

Meditation allows the heart and our subtle energy body to expand and transform; a process through which we come to know Loving-kindness, Empathy and Compassion in a way that upends the ego which, being practical and very much aware of its specific role as mediator between the internal needs of the individual and the outer world, needs encouragement to let go of its shackles. It is the little but impactful gifts of meditation - the glimpses of bliss, the radiance of joy, the growth of wisdom, the feeling of unity with all things - that encourage us to stay on the path even when we encounter setbacks.

During meditation practice when difficulties arise, it is vital to observe the mind's tendency to blame others for our pain, project our short-comings on them and absolve ourselves of any responsibility and so continue the illusion of separateness. The ego re-establishes the status quo and we are back in our deluded comfort zone.

Meditation is our Rosa Mundi[9]; the path which can lead us to the experience of bliss consciousness (Satchitananda). In order to get there, we need to mindfully set about divesting ourselves of our illusions and attempt to move past the conditioned constructs of the ego.

---
[9]Rose/flower of the world.

By bringing mindfulness to our wounds and scary places, we, perchance, may observe our refusal to accept things as they are. Within this process, lies the beginning of the unravelling. If any real benefit is to be had from this exercise, we must allow our observations to stand naked in our awareness without judgement.

All circumstances that seem blocked carry within them the capacity for resolution. We often cannot see our way out because we feel bounded and constrained by our present beliefs as opposed to the limitless freedom of a more wakeful state. If we keep a beginner's mind and remain faithful students, we could use anything that comes up as a means of transformation and see everything as a life lesson or an opportunity to expand the ego and move from separateness into wholeness. Impermanence and change is the nature of the world we live in and patience is an important prerequisite for the journey.

In Buddhist philosophy, the teaching of The Four Sublime Attitudes is an important part of meditation practice and we are encouraged to cultivate the noble, altruistic attitudes of the following qualities in our lives:

- ❖ Loving-kindness or benevolence
- ❖ Compassion
- ❖ Empathetic joy
- ❖ Equanimity

Practising these altruistic, boundless attitudes helps us

to overcome the negative experiences and distressing mental states we endure in the course of our lives, freeing us from the grip of pain, suffering and disenchantment.

The Four Sublime Attitudes are also found in Pantanjali's Yoga Sutras[10] where he encourages us to develop them in meditation and yoga practice and to make them our "treasures and gems which will shine brighter the more we polish them".

Contrary to what organized religions would have us believe, there is no need to seek happiness or spiritual excursions outside of ourselves. All we need for our exploration is to engage with what is already present in ourselves.

We are the guardians of ourselves and the media through which the five elements seek expression. Sometimes the things we feel and experience are not strictly a part of our personal history but emanate out of the collective[11] psyche which all of humanity has inherited and which incorporates patterns of memories, instincts and experiences common to all mankind. These archetypes are observable by their effect on our dreams and behaviours as they move

---

[10] Christopher Chapple (2008) Yoga and the Luminous:Patanjali's Spiritual Path to Freedom

[11] C. G. Jung, The Archetypes and the Collective Unconscious (London 1996)

through us as part of the arising and passing away of our evolutionary process.

Alan Watts has aptly said:

> "we are an aperture through which the universe is expressing itself…"

and through this body-mind phenomena, we can enter into communication with our internal landscape and become intimate with ourselves and our process as we move towards liberation and transcendence.

As we strive to cultivate the bravery of the Warrior, the constancy of the Mountain and the skill of the Dancer, meditation may beckon us, tempting us with the allure of its very worthwhile gifts of integration and synthesis as we learn to dance with the energies that arise and dissipate, for this is truly a Hero's journey.

Breathing

Our breath is our best friend and if we attend it we will have many wonderful adventures together. Right now, as you read this just rest in the breath, receive it effortlessly and feel it leave your body softly, smoothly.

Right here at the tip of our nose, is a key that can unlock a hundred doors. We take approximately 21,000 to 22,000 breaths per day and it all happens through the courtesy of the autonomic nervous system. Nevertheless, respiration can be skillfully controlled by conscious intervention.

The impact of negative emotions can cause over- or under-breathing, the holding of breath and sighing. Changes in the way we breathe are the first response of the body when the little insults of life take place and it accurately reflects our current state of mind. When we are stressed from sitting in traffic, running late for work, anxious about an exam, distressed by an argument with a work colleague or a life partner, we stop breathing properly.

If we bring attention to, and consciously regulate our breathing we can control the emotions. Fear, resentment, agitation, depression, anxiety, impatience, covetousness, grasping and meanness are all reflected in the pattern of our breath. The movement of the mind is revealed in the breath and negative emotions can impact our structure adversely by bringing chronic tension and stresses to our bodies.

The onus is squarely on our shoulders to engage with these energetic patterns *before* they become serious enough to affect our health by learning to breathe properly.

Apart from yoga, the disciplines of psychotherapy, Buteyko breathing, Chi Gong, physiotherapy and mainstream aerobic exercise all offer techniques that can help to get us more in touch with our breath, for the more in touch with our breath we are, the more related to ourselves we become.

Now I will leave you with a couple of breathing techniques that, once you master them, will relax you and keep your respiratory system in good repair.

I have also included a favourite poem of mine which may inspire and enchant you as it did me.

Welcome to the Hero's Journey.

Breathing Technique 1

Learning to breathe from the abdomen is essential to improving control of the emotions and progressing our health.

It is all about letting go ...

softening....

relaxing the shoulders,

bringing your awareness to your breath,

keeping the breath slow and long as you inhale...

feel the body move like a wave as it expands filling the abdomen....pause...

as you exhale slowly, release all the breath gently as you contract the abdomen....

the breath cleanses, purifies and inspires us.

Continue this abdominal breathing for five minutes.

Breathing Technique 2

Another useful tool we can learn to use is the application of lengthening the out-breath, a technique that has many benefits two of which are an increase in stamina and exercise tolerance.

Sit comfortably in loose clothing…

lengthen the spine and drop the shoulders down and back

take your attention to your breath

inhale for a count of six

exhale for a count of twelve, without straining

Repeat

Practise for five minutes.

You Can Never Speak Up Too Often for the Love of All Things

Paul R. Fleischman, M.D.
(An Excerpt)

The silence found throughout the world in evening ponds,
Unbroken forests, mountain-enfolded ravines,
Hilltops at dusk,
Is not an absence of noise, but a presence.
In the company of silence, people hear more clearly the passage of eternity,
Rustling between the lattice of the cells of their own mind,
Like wind through a screen.
In the calm of silence – as if its arms were folded,
and a presence were waiting,
Watching, patiently devoid of impulse or haste –
People hear the common tongue of love, the universal language of mortal things, soft, like a baby's voice,
Passing from person to person, pulsing from
Trees and grass and animals, connecting existence with existence.
Through the universal silent sound of mortal joy, individual life
Becomes bonded, tolerable, and touched.
Aware of this,
You can never speak up too often with the love of all things.

The Yogal Portal

The Yogal Portal

The Yogal Portal

Printed in Great Britain
by Amazon.co.uk, Ltd.,
Marston Gate.